VICTORIAN
RESORTS AND HOTELS

VICTORIAN RESORTS AND HOTELS

Essays from a Victorian Society

Autumn Symposium

EDITED BY

Richard Guy Wilson

Published as Nineteenth Century: Vol. 8, Nos. 1-2, 1982 by
THE VICTORIAN SOCIETY IN AMERICA

© 1982 THE VICTORIAN SOCIETY IN AMERICA

ISSN: 0097-5184

Dr. Richard H. Howland, President, The Victorian Society in America,
East Washinugton Square, Philadelphia, PA 19106. Telephone (215) 627-4252

MEMBERSHIP CATEGORIES FOR 1982

Individual* ($25)   Library/Nonprofit* ($25)   Sustaining ($50)
Contributing ($100)   Life ($1,000)   Benefactor ($5,000).
For further information contact Judith Snyder, Membership Director.
*For membership outside the United States, add $5.

NINETEENTH CENTURY MAGAZINE

Published by The Victorian Society in America for its members, *Nineteenth Century* is devoted to cultural and social history from 1790 to 1917, with feature articles on architecture, fine arts, decorative arts, interior design, lifestyles, preservation, and photography.

TABLE OF CONTENTS

NINETEENTH CENTURY AMERICAN RESORTS AND HOTELS

Richard Guy Wilson

NINETEENTH CENTURY AMERICAN
RESORTS AND HOTELS

Richard Guy Wilson

ICTORIAN RESORTS AND HOTELS always exert a particular fascination—in many ways they define our image of resort and hotel life. The enclosed essays represent the best of the papers presented at the 1979 Victorian Society fall symposium on the topic of "Nineteenth Century Resorts and Hotels." These collected essays do not pretend to be an overall history of the subject, rather they deal with selected aspects and offer new insights into the furnishings, the architects, the buildings, and the manner and means in which Victorians traveled and spent their vacations.

Certainly, the nineteenth century did not invent the resort or the hotel. The origins of both go back into ancient history, for resorts to the Egyptians and Romans escaping from the heat of summer and looking for health-giving waters, and for hotels to inns, guest houses, and any type of accommodation for the traveler and vacationer. But it can be said with very little qualification that during the period of 1820–1914, roughly defined as the Victorian age and its aftermath, that the resort as a specialized activity and the hotel as a building type—whether for the city or the resort—reached the apogee of development. Hotels, resorts, watering places and spas became world wide, from the Grand Hotel at Scarborough, Yorkshire, to the Hotel Byron at Villeneuve, Lake Geneva, and from Shepard's in Cairo to the Astor House Hotel in Shanghai.[1] The role of the United States in this world wide development was central. Americans both visited and imitated foreign hotels and resorts, and at the same time created their own unique varieties and customs.[2] With regard to hotels, Sir Nikolaus Pevsner has written that, beginning with the Tremont House in Boston of 1828–1830, "the United States led the world in hotel building," while another English commentator in 1866 claimed, "The American hotel is to an English hotel what an elephant is to a periwinkle ... An American hotel is as roomy as Buckingham Palace ..."[3] With the resorts, also, Americans have created unique forms that range from Adirondack log cabins decorated in the Japanese style, to high styled hotels along the Florida coast. (*Figures 1 and 2*)

There are a number of ways in which the American development of hotels and resorts can be viewed. They represent an attitude often commented upon, the American penchant for movement and variety. In the nineteenth century Americans were on the road, also, whether for business or pleasure. To meet the need of the traveling and vacationing man, woman, and family, a vast complex of intercity hotels, resorts, and pleasure complexes grew up, from the Isle of Shoals off the New Hampshire Coast, to the other edge of the continent at Coronado, California.

American hotels and resorts also represent the American dream of democratizing old world opulence and luxury. Americans have always striven for the glamor and history of the old world, or as Paul Bourget, a French novelist, wrote after visiting the resort of Newport in 1895, "In this country, where everything is of yesterday, they [Americans] hunger and thirst for the long ago."[4] Available to every man, if he could afford it, was luxury and the association of past ages, even if for just a meal or a night. Certainly there were exclusive resorts. Newport, Rhode Island, is the most famous, yet even here, where "cottages" such as the Breakers cost many millions of dollars, there were hotels, guest houses, and the Casino catering to all classes.

(1) **The Royal Poinciana Hotel, Palm Beach, Florida, 1894, and later additions.** *The Flagler Museum*

(2) **Interior, Adirondack Cabin, 1880s.** *Adirondack Museum*

Money, not class or pedigree, was the entry requirement. The large luxury hotel followed much the same guidelines: if you could pay, anything was possible, and in a country where men rose because of their abilities, it was democratic. Over and over again, reporters and publicists would claim, hotels were "palaces for the public," available to all.[5] The resort and hotel became, then, stage sets in which Americans could act out their fantasies.

Another aspect of the democratic theme is that there were lesser hotels and resorts, not as opulent or as expensive, and that not all Americans sought to emulate European nobility or the American Robber Barons. Resorts from those for "crackers" in Florida, to "tent cities" in California catered to middle and lower classes. These resorts, and ultimately the entire system of hotels and resorts that spanned the nation were only possible with the increasing suburbanization of America and the development of a middle class.

Hotels and resort complexes frequently defined the aspirations of not just the owner and guests, but also the city within which it was located. A large, first class hotel was essential to any city that attempted to attract trade and business and they became in many cases shrines of civic aspirations. The Saint Francis in San Francisco and the Auditorium in Chicago are synonymous with the cities they represent; they were landmarks upon completion. Helena, Montana knew it had arrived when the Hotel Broadwater and Natatorium opened in 1889.

The nineteenth century history of American hotels is a story of increasing functionalism, and also grandeur. Americans led the world in hotel design because they concentrated upon the efficient mechanisms for providing clean rooms, large and edible meals, and silent

(3) Tremont House, Boston, Massachusetts, Dining Room as appeared in 1852. *The Bostonian Society*

unobtrusive service. The result was buildings of tremendous size, luxury and economy, since they fulfilled wants not easily satisfied elsewhere. The earliest American hotels (or at least buildings with that name) appeared in the late eighteenth century, but they were not much more than converted houses although one, The City Hotel in New York, had five floors and seventy-three rooms. Boston tended to lead in the early develment of hotels: Asher Benjamin's Exchange Coffee House, 1806–1809, was a pathbreaker with its 200 guest rooms, elegant series of public rooms, and reported cost of $500,000. Unfortunately it burned in 1818. The most important, though, was Isaiah's Rogers's Tremont House in Boston, 1828–1830, which raised the function of accommodating guests to an art with the elegant and monumental proportions of the building and the excellence of its planning. Elizabeth Jones treats the Tremont House and Rogers's work herewithin, but it is wise to remember that the Tremont was the first hotel to be designed as an architectural monument, and the first to offer to the general public rooms of such noble proportions as the main dining room. (*Figure 3*) From the Tremont there descended a series of noble hotels, the Astor House in New York, 1832–1836, the second Saint Charles in New Orleans, 1851–1853, and the various Gault Houses in Louisville.

The Tremont and its progeny provide the backdrop to the great age of American hotel building in the years 1870–1914. Hotels increased in size, opulence, and associative reference. Styles of architecture from every age and country: Italian *palazzi*, Spanish missions, and English half-timbered country houses, were transformed into hotels. The French Renaissance style became the most popular at the turn-of-the-century as testified to by the long enduring Plaza in New York, the Willard in Washington, D. C., and the Bellevue-Stratford in Philadelphia. The Bellevue-Stratford can be taken as representative of the American luxury hotel at its peak. (*Figures 4 and 5*) Designed by the Philadelphia architectural firm of George W. and W. D. Hewitt, and opened to the public in 1904, the hotel with its 1,090 guest rooms, private baths with curling irons, 700 employees and 1,000 telephones was one of the largest and most opulent. In addition to the usual lobbies and public and private dining rooms and a ballroom, the Bellevue also contained Turkish and Swedish baths, a stockboard and brokers' office, a railroad and steamship ticket office, a florist, a bank, two house orchestras, a theater, and a library. On the exterior, a two-story deeply rusticated limestone base carried an undulating eight-story terra cotta facade topped by a four-story entablature and then five more stories of tall mansard roofs, dormers, iron cresting, and chimney stacks. Over the

(4)   Bellevue-Stratford Hotel, Philadelphia, Pennsylvania, 1904   *Day & Zimmermann Associates*

entire exterior, a rich cladding of French Renaissance-derived ornament added excitement. On the interior, French-styled lobbies and ballroom contrasted with the different-styled guest rooms that included Italian, Greek and Colonial decors. In the lobby, a large clock containing five dial faces to represent different time zones sums up the aspirations and achievement of the Bellevue Hotel: the entire range of human culture and luxury has centered in this hotel in midtown, Philadelphia.

Large hotels such as the Bellevue and its many brethren in the United States constituted a unique way of life for Americans: most at least visited them to gawk if not to stay, and actually many hotels such as the Bellevue had permanent residents. The special nature of American hotel life is testified to in the novels of Edith Wharton, *The House of Mirth* (1905) and *The Custom of the Country* (1913) where she carefully delineates the gradations of hotel society and the daily activities, from the newspaper in the lobby in the morning, to the ritual of the mating game. Henry James, the American expatriot, returned to America in 1904–1905 and found what he called a "hotel spirit:"

You are in the presence of a revelation of the possibilities of the hotel—for which the American spirit has found so unprecedented a use and a value; leading it on to express so a social, indeed positively an aesthetic ideal, and making it so, at this supreme pitch, a synonym for civilization, for the capture of conceived manners themselves, that one is tempted to ask if the hotel spirit may not just be the American spirit most seeking and most finding itself.[6]

The history of resorts parallels in many ways that of hotels, since of course the same building is frequently included, though there are some significant differences. The first American resort, at least for the white man, was probably Stafford Springs, near Hartford, Connecticut, which fashionable Puritans frequented in the seventeenth century.[7] The early history of American resorts is generally a tale of searching for health giving waters, much in the manner of Europeans at Bath and Saint-Moritz, and consequently there is a series of spring resorts in Pennsylvania, Virginia, and of course, Saratoga Springs, New York. The health requirement stayed with many Americans throughout the nineteenth century and still today, ancestors of these early resorts, such as The Homestead at Hot Springs, Virginia, continues this tradition to some degree. However, the health requirement expanded to include the seashore, (*Figure 6*) as indicated by Ahern's paper herewith, and strenuous exercise of hiking and tennis. More importantly, the function of resorts changed from that of health to that of pleasure and luxury, a way of life not available at home. Saratoga Springs, originally a health resort at which the most exciting activities were singing, buggy rides, prayers and taking the waters, became the home of the first temperance society. Consequently, cards, dancing, and lively music along with liquor were banned. About 1820, facing aggressive competition from nearby resorts that catered to the "faster life," the aforementioned activities were reintroduced. Saratoga, as with many resorts, appealed in several areas: relaxation, health, society, and excitement. Other resorts followed with their own special brand of attraction: Cape May and the ocean, the Catskills and the world of nature and scenery. Architecturally, most of these resorts with their hotels and "houses" followed the popular Greek and Italianate styles. The distinguishing features of the hotels was the length and the long veranda or porch, that could in some cases be measured in miles.

For American resorts, the years 1870–1914 saw them also come of age. American energy, expansion and industrial might required the special places, whether Yellowstone or Bar Harbour. The American resort of these

(6)   "The New Venus," TRUTH, Vol. XIV, 13 July 1895, Cover.   *Victorian Society in America*

years has to be seen as an attempt to escape from the pressures, dirt and clamor of the growing American city. The urban population grew nearly fivefold in the years 1870–1910 from nine million to forty-two million, and resorts grew correspondingly. Cultural striving, always present, became the great passion in this period, and the search for civilization and luxury turned the wooden barracks of the earlier resorts hotels into high caloric extravaganzas. Contributing to the great age of American resorts was the development of transportation and also the innovation of vacations—or at least days off. Railroads, interurbans and steam packets opened up the country to resort life. Long Branch New Jersey, quipped a *Harper's* correspondent in 1876, was "the great marine suburb of the great metropolis" of New York, and the same could be said about Atlantic City's relation to Philadelphia.[8] Out of the way places, Mackinac Island and the Grand Hotel, Yellowstone Park and Old Faithful Inn, and the Adirondacks and the Mohonk House, became available to vacations. (*Figure 7*) Henry Morrison Flagler, a former partner of John D. Rockefeller, established a chain of resort hotels down the east

(5) Bellevue-Stratford Hotel, Lobby. *Day &
Zimmerman Associates, Robert Harris photographer*

coast of Florida from Saint Augustine in the north to
the Keys in the south, and linked them with a railroad
that provided the impetus for the subsequent development of the state. Older resorts continued, of course.
Newport, Rhode Island, had been discovered by the
southerners in the 1820s as an escape from the heat of
Savannah and Charleston. They were replaced in the
later 1850s by Boston Brahmans and then in the 1870s
and 1880s, the Bostonians began to retreat as New York
society discovered the town. From the 1880s up to
World War I and even into the 1930s, Newport became the society capital of the United States for the
months of July and August: if you were anybody, an
appearance was mandatory.

Not everybody, of course, went to such high-pow-
ered resorts, and many people in the post-bellum years
rediscovered the virtues of the country and the farm
that their parents may have left 20–30 years ago.[9] Hence
there grew up the farm cottage type of vacation: families would rent rooms from farmers for several weeks
or months. But even this type of vacation became
elaborated and formalized in time, and special buildings, hotels, cottages, and bungalows would be constructed. William Dean Howells's, *The Landlord at
Lion's Head* (1897) gives a picture of a New Hampshire White Mountain farm family, and how the impact of the "summer folks" affects their life. The old
farm house that serves the summer boarders becomes,
in its final incarnation—as described in dialect—a met-
aphor of change:

He'd had one of the leading Boston architects to plan the thing
out. . . . 'Taint's so big as Old Lion's Head, and Jeff want to cater
to a different kind of custom anyway. . . . Know what 'runnay-
sonce' is? Well, that the style Jeff said it was; it's all pillars and
pilasters; and you ride up to the office through a double row of
coluyms, under a kind of portico. It's all painted like them old

15

(7) **Mohonk Mountain House, New Paltz, New York, 1879, additions to 1901.** *Ruth H. Smiley photographer*

Colonial houses down on Brattle Street, buff and white. Well, it made me think of one of them old pagan temples. . . . I wish you could see that dinin'-room o'his: all white colyums and frontin' on the view. Why, that devil's got a regular little theater back ' the dinin'-room for the young folks to act ammyture plays in, and the shows that come along, and he's got a dance-hall besides.[10]

Architecturally, resort hotel designers of the period followed the same eclectic stream as city hotels, though with more freedom of invention. Land with few exceptions (such as Newport) was plentiful and cheap, and the resort hotel could spread out as shown in the aerial view of the Royal Poinciana in Palm Beach. (*Figure 1*) Initially, most of the hotels were of wood in the so-called "Stick style" that was an Americanization of English half-timbering, Italianate, Swiss and French vernacular styles. Framing members would be elaborated and extensive areas of gingerbread would add visual complexity. Then beginning in the late 1870s with the Newport Casino and continuing on into the 1890s, the Shingle Style continued the exploration of the possibilities of wood but with a new sense of con-

tinuity of shapes and surface, rather than the earlier visual multiplication. Created as a synthesis of the English Queen Anne and a new interest in the American past, particularly the seventeenth and early eighteenth New England seacoast architecture, the Shingle style, as it has come to be known (called at the time either Queen Anne or Modernized Colonial) was exclusively a style of the resort.[11] Later it would be adapted to suburbia and country houses. The Hotel Del Coronado (treated by Kantor herewithin) represents the high point of the style. William Dean Howells, always a close observer of American life, described in a novel the "summer settlement" of the 1880s as:

A strange world—a world of colonial and Queen Anne architecture, where conscious lines and insistent colours contributed to an effect of posing . . . never seen off the stage.. . . .In detail it was not so bad now, but the whole was a violent effect of porches, gables, chimneys, loggias, balconcies, and jalousies, which nature had not yet had time to palliate.[12]

In the later 1880s a sense of formality, stability and monumentality was introduced into the resort hotel idiom. Materials became more permanent than wood and stylistic references are to later eighteenth century American Colonial, English classical, and the entire range of European Renaissance architecture. Henry

16

(8) Ponce de Leon Hotel, Saint Augustine, Florida,
      1885-88. *Historical Society of Palm Beach County*

(9) Ponce de Leon Hotel, Rotunda. *The Flagler
      Museum*

Morrison Flagler's Ponce de Leon in Saint Augustine
Florida, 1885–1888, represents well the new type of
resort hotel. (*Figures 8 and 9*) Designed by the New
York architects John Mervin Carrère and Thomas Hast-
ings, recent graduates of the McKim, Mead & White
office and the Ecole des Beaux Arts, they were assisted
by another recent Ecole graduate, Bernard Maybeck.
Permanence was achieved by the use of concrete and
the Ponce de Leon was the first large cast concrete
structure in the United States. Stylistically, it recalled
the Spanish Renaissance with the towers, tile roofs, and
terra cotta and molded brick ornament, but with a freedom of reference and lushness that made the entire
setting into an exotic, far-away, never-never land, suddenly come to life. Lions of Leon served as lamp standards and wall sconces with light bulbs clutched in
their teeth. Doorknobs were modeled after sea shells.
Beyond the large entrance garden court filled with
fountains and greenery, lay the rotunda, decorated with

carved oak columns and topped by a dome with allegorical paintings by George Maynard and glass by Louis Comfort Tiffany. Containing 450 guest suites, though strangely no private bathrooms, the Ponce de Leon was soon joined by another Flagler hotel, the Alcazar. Together they became for a period the winter headquarters of the cream of American society and led the way for Florida to become the winter playground for Americans.

The recently destroyed Marlborough-Blenheim Hotel, 1905–1906, in Atlantic City, New Jersey, represents the high point of American resort hotel design. (Figure 10) Designed by the Philadelphia firm of Price and McLanahan, who were responsible for numerous other resort hotels, the Marlborough picks up on the contemporary English Edwardian Baroque idiom—indicative of its name—and uses a new ornamental language of shells, mermaids, seaweed and seahorses. The rich diversity of its many parts, the cupolas, chimney stacks, and dome, are integrated into a unified expression that differentiates American architecture of the turn-of-the-century period from the earlier visual multiplicity of buildings from the mid-century. Atlantic City, in spite of boasting as a resort of the elite, was always the "Meccas of Millions," and much more a middle class and working men's resort.[13] The Marlborough-Blenheim brought the richness of the old world to the boardwalk.

Around resorts, as with city hotels, a unique life style grew up: dozing on the porch in the morning, the afternoon tea dance, the gala ball at night. Activities varied with the resort and the money involved, exercise might be archery on the lawn, croquet, or gin-rummy, but the intent was to escape the cares of the workaday world.

* * *

The centrality of hotels and resorts to an understanding of nineteenth century American culture cannot be overestimated. They defined ways of life and standards for many Americans. Of equal interest, resorts and hotels have left us with a rich artistic and intellectual heritage, and in many ways some of the major themes of the nineteenth century. Their architectural importance goes without saying. Mention has been made of the writings of Henry James and Edith Wharton on hotels; the resort played an equally large role in their works. William Dean Howells, an astute chronicler of the middle class, saw the resort and the city hotel as indicative of changes in America. And of course there were many other writers who could be noted: Nathaniel Hawthorne, Julia Ward Howe, Thomas Wentworth Higginson, and Mrs. Trollope.

(11)   "On the Bluff at Long Branch, at the Bathing Hour," HARPER'S WEEKLY, 6 August 1879. *Winslow Homer*

Painters, especially, were attracted by resorts, and in some cases led the way in their establishment. Many of the great landscape paintings of the Hudson River and Luminist Schools that are admired so much as representing an American vision are really products of resort life. Thomas Cole's, *The Notch of the White Mountains*, 1839 (National Gallery, Washington, D. C.) is a summer resort painting. Many of Martin Johnson Heade's and John Kennsett's ocean and marsh scenes that catch the changes of light, the stillness of the water, or a gathering storm, were done at Newport or other New England seacoast resorts. Summer colonies of painters and artists grew up, from Stockbridge and Lenox in the Berkshires, the Cos Cob School in Connecticut, and Carmel on the West Coast. Finally, many of Winslow Homer's works, either in paintings or prints, are about the summer resort spirit, as the many views of tourists on Mount Washington, or *On the Bluff at Long Branch, At the Bathing Hour*, will indicate.   (*Figure 11*)

Today, for the most part, nineteenth century hotels and resorts are either destroyed or completely changed. Americans in the later twentieth century seem not to demand the trappings of culture as did their nineteenth century ancestors. Overnight lodging is in the pitifully pretentious and euphemistically named Holiday Inn. The idea of a resort still remains, but with new twists as thoughts of Las Vegas, Miami, and the Playboy Resort Hotel will indicate. The reasons for the change go far beyond the intent of this essay. Still, though, there are survivors—as indicated by the Grand Hotel on Mackinac Island, the Mohonk Mountain House in New Paltz, and the Bellevue-Stratford in Philadelphia.

(10) Marlborough-Blenheim Hotel, Atlantic City, New Jersey, 1905-1906. *William J. McCrea photographer*

The recent restoration of the Bellevue offers a glimmer of a brighter future.[14] Changed though we are, the resorts and hotels of the nineteenth century exercise a hold on us and call us back.

NOTES

[1] Robert B. Ludy, *Historic Hotels of the World* (Philadelphia, 1927).

[2] Jefferson Williamson, *The American Hotel: An Anecdotal History* (New York, 1930); Jeffery Limerick, Nancy Ferguson and Richard Oliver, *America's Grand Resort Hotels* (New York, 1979); and Roger Hale Newton, "Our Summer Resort Architecture—An American Phenomenon and Social Document," *American Quarterly* 41 (Autumn 1941), pp. 297–318.

[3] Nikolaus Pevsner, *A History of Building Types* (London, 1976), pp. 176, 182.

[4] Paul Bourget, *Outre-Mer: Impressions of America* (New York, 1895), p. 53.

[5] Doris Elizabeth King, "The First Class Hotel and Age of the Common Man," *Journal of Southern History*, XXIII (May 1957), p. 180.

[6] Henry James, *The American Scene* (New York, 1946), p. 102.

[7] Cleveland Amory, *The Last Resorts* (New York, 1952), p. 17.

[8] Olive Logan, "Life at Long Branch," *Harper's* 53 (September 1876), pp. 481–822.2

[9] John Burroughs, "Picturesque Aspects of Farm Life in New York," *Scribner's Monthly Magazine*, 17 (November 1878), pp. 41–54.

[10] William Dean Howells, *The Landlord At Lion's Head* (New York, 1897), p. 448.

[11] Vincent Scully, Jr., *The Shingle Style and the Stick Style*, revised edition (New Haven, 1971); Richard Guy Wilson, "The Early Work of Charles F. McKim: Country House Commissions," *Winterthur Portfolio*, 14 (Autumn 1979), pp. 235–67.

[12] William Dean Howells, *Annie Kilburn* (New York, 1889), pp. 105–106.

[13] Limerick, et al. *America's Grand Resort Hotels*, p. 159.

[14] The architect for the restoration/renovation of the Bellevue-Stratford was Hyman Myers, AIA, of Day & Zimmermann Associates of Philadelphia.

FOREIGN TRAVELLERS AND AMERICAN HOTELS

John Maass

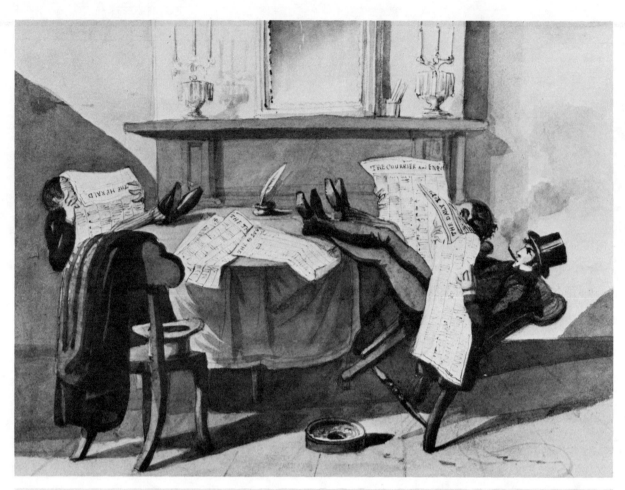

FOREIGN TRAVELLERS AND AMERICAN HOTELS

John Maass

IN OCTOBER 1860 a young Victorian gentleman told the Mayor of New York that his accommodations at the Fifth Avenue Hotel were more comfortable than his rooms at home. His home was Buckingham Palace, for this was Victoria's son, the Prince of Wales. He did, however, not tell that to his mother but wrote to her only: "After arriving at our hotel we were very glad to get our dinner and go to bed, as we had a very tiring day." [1] When the future Edward VII praised his American hotel, he was in keeping with countless visitors to the U.S. during the Victorian era. The hotel was, of course, an institution of European origin. Many American hotels sought to convey distinction by their European names—Windsor, Westminster, Buckingham, Clarendon, Vendome, Touraine, Savoy and the like. Yet, many foreign travellers declared that American hotelkeepers had in some respects beaten the Europeans at their own game. There are hundreds of published reports by foreign visitors, and I present as many excerpts as space permits. I have arranged them in chronological order and let the travellers speak in their own words.

* * *

1837 The popular English novelist Captain Frederick Marryat arrived in New York a month before Victoria's accession. His *Diary in America* has an enthusiastic chapter "Hostelry and Gastronomy." The American "mania for travelling" demanded that "everything connected with locomotion should be well arranged ...

therefore, it is so." Marryat was delighted by the hotels' enormous menus and bars with

masses of pure crystal ice, large bunches of mint, decanters of every sort of wine, every variety of spirits, lemons, sugar, bitters ... It really makes one thirsty, even the going into a bar.

He was, however, disgusted by the "ridiculous pretended modesty" of American women whenever one of their own sex arrived "of whom some little scandal has been afloat." They bullied their husbands and the proprietor until the "libelled parties" were requested to leave the hotel. [2]

1842 Charles Dickens made a lecture tour. Young, handsome and already famous, he was lionized everywhere but repaid hospitality with endless faultfinding in letters and his book *American Notes*. In Boston he mistook the wardrobe in his hotel room for a "showerbath." In Philadelphia he arrived late and complained because he was charged for the days his rooms had been reserved. He constantly raged about the custom of spitting:

In every bar-room and hotel passage the stone floor looks as if it were paved with open oysters—from the quantity of this kind of deposit which tesselates it all over.

He liked the Planter's House in St. Louis:

The inns in these outlandish corners of the world would astonish you by their goodness ... They had the famous notion of sending up at breakfast-time large glasses of new milk with blocks of ice in them ... One day when we were dining in our own room, we counted sixteen dishes on the table at the same time. [3]

1847 The Argentine educator Domingo Sarmiento saw an American rage for travel: "Judgment Day would surprise two thirds of the population on the road like ants." He marvelled at the riverboats, floating hotels with bridal suites where "rose-tinted lamps burn, and flowers and aromatic essences sharpen the privileged tenants' appetite for pleasure." Like other foreigners he

---

(1) Reading Room, Astor House, New York. Watercolor Drawing by Nicolino V. Calyo, c. 1840. *Museum of the City of New York*

(2) St. Charles Hotel, New Orleans. Lithograph by S. W. Thayer & Son, 1845. *Louisiana State Museum*

noted that "four persons seated about a marble-topped table will invariably rest their eight feet on it unless they can find a seat upholstered in velvet." (*Figure 1*) At the sound of a gong the Yankees rush to hotel dining rooms. They set aside two minutes for lunch, five minutes for dinner, and the noise of plates, knives and scraping chairs can be heard half a mile away. Approaching New Orleans, he saw a dome which reminded him of St. Peter's in Rome. He was surprised to find that it was the St. Charles Hotel: (*Figure 2*)

Now I believe in the republic, in democracy, in everything; I forgive the Puritans, even the one who ate raw tomato sauce with the tip of his knife and before the soup. Everything should be forgiven to the people who erect monuments to the dining room and crown the kitchen with a cupola like this.[4]

1851 The French author J. J. Ampère resolved to study not American "monuments" but "institutions and people." In New Orleans he found the vast St. Charles "a curiosity." As the son of the great physicist A. M. Ampère, he was intrigued by an "electro-magnetic apparatus" in the rooms:

By pressing a button one interrupts the current, and the room number disappears from a board in the lobby; a bell is struck at the same time . . . In this country science is not only applied to industry but employed for the most ordinary services. Instead of pulling a bell cord, one brings into play a battery![5]

1851 The French pianist Henri Herz also admired the St. Charles:

A tremendous structure surmounted by a dome, modelled after our Panthéon in Paris . . . I was told (I did not count them myself) that there were 2,000 rooms in that caravanserai . . . Fire, the great national scourge, has since consumed the hotel.

He stayed at a small New Orleans hotel owned by a quadroon lady. He saw the proprietress lower a slave girl into the well to punish her. Herz stopped this "humid vengeance" by threatening to move from a house "where I court the danger of drinking water which has served as a bath for Negresses."[6]

1853 W. M. Thackeray stayed at some of the same hotels as Dickens but had no complaints. When the gas was turned off at the Clarendon in New York while he was writing a letter, he calmly continued, "but there's light enough by my midnight taper."[7]

1860 The greatest Victorian traveller, Richard Burton, visited Utah to write a book, *The City of the Saints*: "In the Far West one learns not to expect too much of the hostelry" but the Mormon owner of the rough looking Salt Lake House "was in the highest degree civil and obliging, attended personally to our wants, and put us all in the best of humours."[8]

(4) At the Continental Hotel, Philadelphia. *Wood Engraving from George Augustus Sala, America Revisited, 1883*

1860 A Japanese mission toured the U. S. The envoys greatly admired America but were puzzled by quaint occidental customs in hotels. At the Willard in Washington one mistook "a clean white jar under the bed" for a head rest. Americans bathed alone and behind locked doors. American women were attractive but immodest, baring their necks and shoulders: "In this country women are more precious than men. For example, whenever there are not enough chairs, men stand up and women take the seats." At balls, men and women "went round and round like white mice." (*Figure 3*) The polite Japanese always ate their dinners but disliked the "greasy" food; they enjoyed a dessert that melted in the mouth (ice cream). The visitors, "accustomed to the quiet manners observed at our banquets," were "deafened" by the noise of popping champagne bottles and clapping hands.[9]

1867 On his second visit, Dickens took care to be less critical. The Parker House in Boston was

an immense hotel, with all manner of white marble public rooms. I live in a corner high up, have a hot and cold bath in my bedroom, and comforts not in existence when I was here before. The cost of living is enormous, but happily we can afford it.[10]

1868 Sarmiento returned as the Argentine Minister to the U. S. At the Continental in Philadelphia

I had to be conducted three times to my rooms, lost in that colossal labyrinth until they showed me the furnished room that takes you from the first floor to the seventh, letting off at intermediate floors passengers who go up and down sitting on soft seats.

After "the three happiest years of his life" in the U. S. Sarmiento was elected President of Argentina.[11]

(3) **Ball for the Japanese Embassy at the Metropolitan Hotel, New York.** *Wood Engraving from Harper's Weekly, 1860*

1876 The French composer Jacques Offenbach stayed at a New York hotel with "an immense bazaar, a city of merchants" on the ground floor. One could enter "naked as Adam and hairy as Absalom" and leave dressed in the height of fashion. The menu listed no less than eighty *plats du jour*. He thought it "comic" that all dishes ordered were brought at the same time.[12]

1876 Dr. Georg Seelhorst, a Bavarian museum official, found even small hotels excellent:

The dinner menu of a hotel in Williamsport, Pa., a city of 18,000, enumerated 3 soups, 3 kinds of fish, 4 kinds of boiled meat, 5 cold meats, 6 steamed 'entrees', 5 roasts, 11 vegetables, 14 side dishes and 21 desserts! This abundance is of course considerably surpassed in large hotels . . . It is not proper to drink beer or wine with it; ice water is the only drink for those who do not want tea.[13]

1876 The Polish journalist Henryk Sienkiewicz also criticized the American way of serving:

You have before you all at one time, soup, meat, fish, eggs, puddings, tomatoes, potatoes, ice cream, strawberries, apples, almonds, coffee . . . As a result, everything you eat is cold, stale and unappetizing.

In Chicago, the Palmer House was

An edifice built of huge marble slabs in true Babylonian magnificence. Everything within simply drips with gold, silk and velvet. My eyes blinked under the brilliant lights . . . Indeed, this hotel is the most remarkable sight in town.

He was surprised that even unmarried American women travelled without chaperons and dined in hotels without escorts.[14]

1876 The Polish actress Helena Modjeska noted "the singular custom of men sitting in rocking chairs and putting their feet on window sills in hotel lobbies . . . Wherever you turn, these soles stare at you."[15]

1879 Ernst Hesse-Wartegg, an Austrian writer of travel books, noted the vast "floating population" in the U. S.:

Hundreds of thousands of Americans spend their entire lives in hotels. They are always on a hunt. The quarry is the Dollar; it may hide in the manufacture of improved trouser buttons, in a Colorado gold mine, in a Southern cotton plantation, in a new steamship line. As soon as the hunter hears the news, his travelling trunk is packed. Everywhere there are great hotels for these roving people.[16]

1880 The French star Sarah Bernhardt received special treatment from hotel owners who knew the value of good publicity. At the Albermarle in New York her suite was decorated with palms, flowers and busts of Racine, Molière and Victor Hugo. In Chicago, Potter Palmer of the Palmer House, "a perfect gentleman, courteous, kind and generous, taxed his ingenuity to have me served in the French style, a rare thing at that time." [17]

1882 The English journalist Charles Augustus Sala wrote about hotels with relish. At the Continental in Philadelphia the breakfast bill of fare included:

Boiled, fried, poached, 'dropped' and scrambled eggs, omelettes of every style, fried, stewed, and roasted oysters, hashed codfish with cream, fishballs, dried and smoked salmon and herrings, salt mackerel, fresh fish in season, mutton chops, beefsteaks, pork cutlets, sausages, ham, bacon, cold meat, chicken, tea, coffee, and chocolate, a variety of fancy bread, including 'waffles', buckwheat cakes, and, to crown it all, a copious dessert—remember, we were in mid-December—of apples, Californian, oranges, fresh Malaga grapes, and bananas . . . For dinner, the menu is more varied. (Figure 4)

Sala met a "mild and unobtrusive-looking gentleman":

The proprietor of the Continental Hotel in Philadelphia! The Admiral commanding Noah's Ark, the landlord of the Mammoth Cave, the 'Boss' of the Tower of Babel and the Hanging Gardens of Babylon, rather. Why was he not 120 feet high, and the very least? Why did he not have a guard of halberdiers, or of Varangian cross-bowmen? Why was he not accompanied by a Grand Vizier, a Kislar Aga, a Sheikh-ul-Islam, and several Bimbashis?

At the Grand Pacific in Chicago, there were "gorgeous hotel clerks" who looked like "Croesus-cum-Rothschild, German Grand Dukes travelling incognito, officers commanding regiments of the Household Cavalry." He had an "alcove bedroom":

Height at least fifteen feet; two immense plate-glass windows; beautiful frescoed ceiling; couch, easy chairs, rocking chairs, foot stools in profusion, covered with crimson velvet; large writing table for gentleman, pretty escritoire for lady; two towering cheval glasses; commanding pier glass over mantelpiece; adjoining bathroom beautifully fitted; rich carpet; and finally the bed, in a deep alcove, impenetrably screened by elegant lace curtains. Now I call that a bedroom, and no mistake . . . With the exception of the St. Pancras in London and the Continental in Paris, I have seen no more splendid hotel in the world.

San Francisco, "The Bay City," might as well be called "The Bay Window City," the "magnificent" new Palace, (Figure 5) Grand and Baldwin Hotels had facades "corrugated" with bay windows. Sala summed up:

While travelling in America never cease to bear this cardinal fact in mind, that this is a wholesale and not a retail country. Everything is on an extensive scale. Nothing is petty.[18] (Figure 6)

1883 Friedrich von Hellwald, a German author of travel books, visited several resorts. In Newport

The three hotels eke out a bare existence. Despite their watery names—Ocean House, Aquidneck and Atlantic—they are inland. To stay by the sea without seeing it is surely the greatest sacrifice. Instead of the splendid hotels of other seaside resorts Newport has something far better: 600–700 elegant private residences which have hardly an equal elsewhere.

He found that Atlantic City had no right to its proud name. It was a dull place with dust in the streets and flies in the hotels, "almost the exclusive property of Philadelphians, and just as boring as the Quaker City itself." Quite different was "cheerful" Cape May. (Figure 7) It had a "Ladies' Mile," a boardwalk between the fashionable main avenue and the surf:

This is the great promenade, the rendezvous of Senators and Congressmen from Washington, and the money-aristocracy of Baltimore and Philadelphia. In a quarter of an hour you can here see America's most beautiful women: truly junoesque figures with the most charming faces, luxuriant hair and splendid eyes. In its great hotels Cape May offers all desired comforts.

In Chicago, the Tremont, Palmer House, Grand Pacific and Sherman vied for the honor of being "the premier hotel of the world." They were palaces, even more lavish than the hotels of Saratoga. In San Francisco, "the highly praised Palace Hotel, which can house 1,200 guests, consists of so many windows that it resembles a colossal cage." [19]

1889 On another journey Hesse-Wartegg visited the "Temperance State" of Rhode Island. It was illegal to sell alcoholic beverages but there was no law against giving them away. The resort hotels of Newport and Narragansett Pier had an understanding with the authorities: They served wines and liquors without charge; the cost then appeared as "Extras" on the guest's weekly bill. Hesse-Wartegg knew the famous Palace and Baldwin Hotels of San Francisco. In Seattle, "a telegraphing, telephoning, electrified Yankee city in a forest wilderness," he stayed at a large hotel with "splendid rooms and all modern facilities." But the finest hotel on the Pacific was the "comfortable, Old English, quiet" Driard House in Victorian Victoria, British Columbia. 6,000 miles from London, he saw gentlemen and ladies in full evening dress having champagne in a dining room adorned with oil paintings; in the reading room "four light blonde Misses in black silk stockings" were leafing through English magazines. The owner was Austrian, the building of the adjoining Victoria Theatre was Hungarian, the chef was French, the kitchen staff Italian, the waiters English, and instead of chambermaids there were pigtailed young Chinese men.[20]

(5) Palace Hotel, San Francisco.   Wood Engraving
     from George Augustus Sala, America Revisited, 1883

(6) **The Colonnade of a Large American Hotel.** *Wood Engraving from George Augustus Sala, America Revisited, 1883*

1891 The Polish pianist Ignace Paderewski "spent a dreadful night" at the Union Square Hotel in New York: "There were spots black with a mass of insects." The firm of Steinway then paid for rooms at the Windsor, "a very old-fashioned but comfortable hotel with good food." [21]

1906 The Russian writer Maxim Gorky arrived in New to raise money for revolutionaries. He was welcomed by many prominent Americans. The Czar's embassy then leaked to the press that "the charming Madame Gorky" was really a Madame Andreyeva (Gorky was separated from his wife). The proprietor of the Belleclaire exclaimed: "This is not Europe– I am running a family hotel, and I cannot have these people in my house any longer." In the next two days Gorky and his companion were also evicted from the Lafayette-Brevoort and Rhinelander Hotels. They had to move in with friends. [22]

1909 The famous Baedeker guide *The United States* was written for British travellers by an English editor, J. F. Muirhead. In New York some hotels were themselves among the great sights:

Strangers who do not put up at any of the largest and most gorgeous hostelries should at least visit one of them to obtain an idea of their lavish decorations and elaborate contrivances for convenience and comfort . . . Among the most notable houses are the Waldorf-Astoria (mural paintings), the Astor (largest kitchen in the world), the new Plaza, the Knickerbocker, the St. Regis (mural decorations and Flemish tapestry), the Gotham, and the Manhattan (mural paintings).

In Philadelphia, the Baedeker recommended the *Bellevue-Stratford, "a huge edifice resembling the Waldorf-Astoria in New York which is under the same management. Rooms from $2½." In San Francisco, the *Fairmont was "a colossal structure with a fine outlook. Rooms from $3." Saratoga Springs was a popular watering-place "in spite of its want of fine scenery." A visit to the enormous ball-rooms, dining-rooms and piazzas of the United States Hotel and the Grand Union "should not be omitted." A complete contrast was the Methodist resort of Ocean Grove, New Jersey:

This extraordinary settlement, possible only in America, in which many thousands of people, young and old, voluntarily elect to spend their summer vacations under a religious autocracy, which is severe both in its positive and negative regulations, is curious enough to repay a short visit.

Among resort hotels singled out by the Baedeker were the Catskill Mountain House with a **View "of unique beauty and interest"; the *Ponce de Leon and the Alcazar in St. Augustine, both "in the Spanish

(7) "The Humors of Cape May." *Wood Engravings from Harper's Weekly, 1871*

Renaissance style"; the *El Tovar on the rim of the **Grand Canyon; the "delightfully situated" *Hotel del Coronado where "the flower-beds are of astonishing brilliancy." [23]

1909 Prof. Sigmund Freud spent four weeks in the U. S. At Niagara he was miffed when a tourist guide called out, "let the old fellow go first" (Freud was 53). He blamed American cooking for an attack of appendicitis, and complained to his biographer about rest rooms: "They escort you along miles of corridors and ultimately you are taken to the very basement where a marble palace awaits you, just in time." [24]

* * *

There is remarkable unanimity among the foreign visitors' reports. They always describe the "American Plan" in which the price of the hotel room included four or even five meals a day. They invariably comment on the "colored help" as they were unaccustomed to see Blacks *en masse* or in "European clothes." They are amazed by the quantity and variety of food and drink. They note that many American families have permanently moved into hotels because it is hard to find household servants in egalitarian America. They marvel at the scale, wealth, speed, efficiency, material comforts and modern conveniences of the U. S. They admire the big-hearted, friendly, informal, enterprising, hospitable and chivalrous Americans who are always on the move —or they abhor the crude, loud, vulgar, hustling, rootless, money-grubbing and henpecked Yankees who are always on the make. Did the hotels form this familiar image of the U. S.? Or did the hotels merely confirm preconceived notions? In any case, the foreign travellers regarded the hotel as America in microcosm.

NOTES

[1] Sir Sidney Lee, *King Edward VII* (London, 1925), 1.

[2] Frederick Marryatt, *A Diary in America* (London, 1839).

[3] Charles Dickens, *Letters 1842* (London, 1965).

[4] Domingo Sarmiento, *Travels in the United States in 1847* (Princeton, 1970).

[5] J. J. Ampère, *Promenade en Amérique* (Paris, 1856).

[6] Henri Herz, *Mes Voyages en Amérique* (Paris, 1866).

[7] *The Letters and Private Papers of William Makepeace Thackeray* (New York, 1945).

[8] Richard Burton, *The City of the Saints* (New York, 1862).

[9] Foster Rhea Dulles, *Yankees and Samurai* (New York, 1965). Tadashi Aruga, "The First Japanese Mission to the United States," in Marc Pachter (Ed.), *Abroad in America* (Washington, 1976).

[10] Charles Dickens, *Letters 1867* (London, 1965).

[11] A. W. Bunkley, *A Life of Sarmiento* (Princeton, 1952).

[12] Jacques Offenbach, *Offenbach en Amérique* (Paris, 1876).

[13] Georg Seelhorst, *Die Philadelphia-Weltausstellung und was sie lehrt* (Nördlingen, 1878).

[14] Henryk Sienkiewicz, *Portrait of America* (New York, 1959).

[15] Helena Modjeska, *Memories and Impressions* (New York, 1910).

[16] Ernst Hesse-Wartegg, *Amerika* (Leipzig, 1879).

[17] Sarah Bernhardt, *Memoirs of my Life* (New York, 1907).

[18] Charles Augustus Sala, *America Revisited* (London, 1883).

[19] Friedrich von Hellwald, *Amerika in Wort und Bild* (Leipzig, n.d., c. 1883).

[20] Ernst Hesse-Wartegg, *Curiosa aus der Neuen Welt* (Leipzig, 1893).

[21] Ignacy Jan Paderewski and Mary Lawton, *The Paderewski Memoirs* (New York, 1927).

[22] Alexander Kaun, *Maxim Gorki and his Russia* (New York, 1931).

[23] Karl Baedeker, *The United States* (London, 1909).

[24] Ernest Jones, *The Life and Work of Sigmund Freud* (New York, 1953–57), Vol. 2.

HOTEL DESIGN IN THE WORK OF
ISAIAH ROGERS AND HENRY WHITESTONE

Elizabeth Fitzpatrick Jones

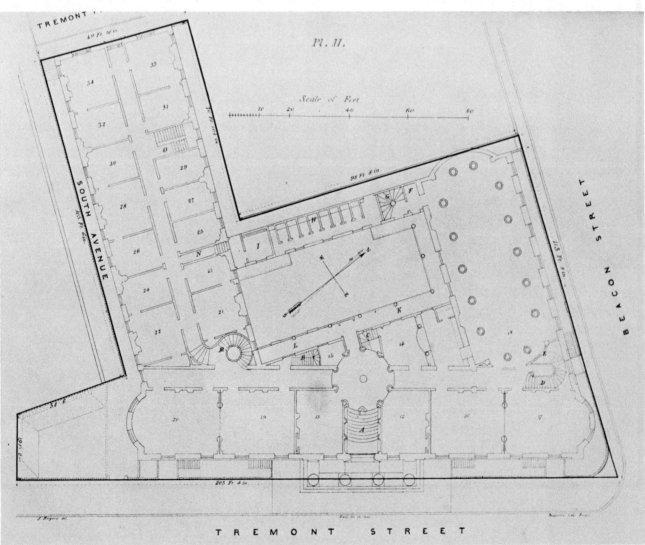

Pl. II.

Scale of Feet

SOUTH AVENUE

BEACON STREET

TREMONT STREET

HOTEL DESIGN IN THE WORK OF
ISAIAH ROGERS AND HENRY WHITESTONE

Elizabeth Fitzpatrick Jones

LOUISVILLE, with its strategic location at the
Falls of the Ohio, has always been a stopping
point for travelers. After the invention of the
steamboat and the opening of the Portland Canal at
the Falls in 1830, Louisville needed to expand its hotel
facilities. In 1832, the Louisville Hotel advertised its
debut and by 1835, the Galt House opened its doors.

At mid-century, Louisville was continuing its growth
and with the advent of the Louisville and Nashville
Railroad more hotel space was needed. Isaiah Rogers
and his Irish-born partner Henry Whitestone, were
hired to redesign the Galt House and the Louisville
Hotel.

During the nineteenth century many changes were
wrought in architectural styles and technology. A most
visible metamorphosis was in the design of the hotel.
The singular hotel which was responsible for this
change was the Tremont House in Boston.

The Tremont House was designed by Isaiah Rogers
(1800–1869). Rogers, who was born on a farm near
Plymouth, Mass., was the son of a ship builder. At the
age of sixteen, Rogers apprenticed himself to a house
carpenter. In 1826, after spending four years in the
office of Solomon Willard (1783–1861), Rogers opened
an office in Boston, and in 1828, received the commission for the Tremont House, which was to revolutionize
hotel design. Rogers designed numerous hotels all over
the United States. His designs included the Astor House
in New York, the second St. Charles House in New
Orleans, the Battle House in Mobile, the Charleston
Hotel in Charleston, and the Burnet House in Cincinnati. Rogers was responsible for numerous buildings
other than hotels, including the completion of the Ohio
State Capitol in 1858–60. From 1862 through 1865, he
was Supervising Architect for the Treasury Department.[1]
The success of the Tremont House can be attributed
to its originality in comparison with the inns and lodging houses available for travelers in 1830. (*Figure 1*)

The many heretofore unheard-of services which
were provided, the size of the structure, and the various
conveniences all contributed to making the Tremont
House a landmark in the history of hotels. Unfortunately, the structure was demolished ca. 1895. A
monograph on the building with drawings and eleva-
tions was published in 1830,[2] and influenced hotel design in the United States. (*Figure 2*) The preface to
the study stated:

The present publication is intended to satisfy a curiosity, which
frequent inquiries for a description of Tremont House were supposed to indicate.

Its original plan was to furnish such particulars relative to
this establishment as strangers might wish to possess, but it has
been extended so as to comprehend many architectural details,
which will probably be interesting to mechanics; since the design
of the principal parts of the ornamental work of Tremont House,
either as precise copies or general imitations, were derived from
books not easy to be obtained, and have not before been executed in this country. The account given of the attempt which
has been made in this edifice to remedy some of the ordinary
defects of construction in large public houses; by means hitherto
unknown or not used in Boston, and the advantage of examining
the execution of what is here illustrated, will no doubt be
thought to give additional utility to this publication.[3]

The published description conveys the importance
of the Tremont House, "Since the destruction of the
old Exchange Coffee House in 1818, no hotel had been
built in this city on a scale of equal extent with that
structure...."[4] "The general effect of the exterior of
Tremont House is imposing from its magnitude and its

---

(1)   The Tremont House, Boston, Mass. Demolished,
      *W. H. Eliot, A Description of the Tremont House,
      Boston: 1830*

(2)   Plan of the Tremont House.   *W. H. Eliot, A
      Description of the Tremont House, Boston: 1830*

just proportions; and the selection and execution of the decorated parts of the facade exhibit the classical taste of the Architect, and his judicious adherence to the established principles of Grecian Architecture." [5]

Rogers was the first architect with whom Henry Whitestone (1819–1893), is known to have come in contact in the United States. Whitestone was born in Ireland at Clondegad House, Ballynacally, County Clare. Although his family was English, his ancestors had been in County Clare since 1667. According to oral tradition, Whitestone was educated at the University of Dublin, Trinity College. Records of Trinity College indicate that Whitestone was never enrolled there, but his brother was a graduate of the institution. The source of Whitestone's architectural training is not known. Several sources credit him with having been the architect of the County Courthouse at Ennis, County Clare, constructed ca. 1840–1850. A Dublin Architect, J. B. Keane was alledgedly paid for a design for the Courthouse at Ennis. Whitestone could have apprenticed under Keane in Dublin and become Supervising Architect under Keane for the Courthouse and has thus been credited with the design.[6]

According to a diary kept by Whitestone's brother, Henry had left Ireland for America in January of 1852 after marrying. He had probably left Ireland because of the situation as recorded in an 1850 article in *The Builder*, which said, "The principal causes of the present low state of architectural practice in Ireland is certainly the poverty of the country..." [7] Whitestone brought with him a letter of introduction from Crofton Vandeleur, M. P. from West Clare, to the right Honorable Abbott Lawrence (1792–1855) former U. S. Minister to Great Britain. Whether Whitestone used this letter (or not) is unknown; it is still in the possession of his heirs.[8]

Whitestone was associated with Rogers by July of 1852, according to Rogers' diary and by October of 1852, Whitestone was at work on "Finished Plans" for the Frankfort, Kentucky Hotel (later known at the Capital Hotel).[9] By 1853, Whitestone was in Louisville, Kentucky working with Rogers on the enlargement of the old Galt House. Rogers and Whitestone were partners until 1857, with Rogers in Cincinnati and Whitestone in Louisville. Both were responsible for numerous commissions. Whitestone is best known for his sumptuous but restrained residences in the Renaissance Revival mode and for his commercial structures.[10]

Rogers and Whitestone's first joint endeavor was the Capital Hotel in Frankfort, Kentucky. The stone exterior of the Capital Hotel was more Roman than Greek, and it was much more ornate than the earlier Tremont House. The Burnet House (*Figure 3*) in

(3) The Burnet House, Cincinnati, Ohio. Demolished. Cincinnati in 1851, *Cincinnati, 1851*

(4) The Capital Hotel, Frankfort, KY. Demolished. *Kentucky Historical Society, Frankfort, Kentucky*

Cincinnati (1850) and the Capital Hotel seem to have benefited from Rogers' knowledge of the series of drawings executed for the "Park" or "Astor" Hotel in New York in 1832, by the firm of Town and Davis.[11] The Capital had a hexastyle Corinthian portico with projecting wings on either side. The center of the roof was marked by a low sixteen-sided cupola with narrow arched windows. The cupola resembled the drum of a dome, but there is no dome above it. (*Figure 4*)

Whitestone came to Louisville, Kentucky in 1853, after his sojourn in Frankfort. His first work in Louisville was in conjunction with Rogers on the enlargement of the old Galt House. The first Galt House had been built in ca. 1835, at Second and Main Streets on the site of the house of a well-known physician, Dr. Wm. C. Galt. The hotel was a simple rectangle with a hipped roof, a shape not unlike the Tremont House, although the Galt House was not so finely detailed and the architect is unknown. Charles Dickens had stayed at the Galt House in 1842, and praised it saying, "We slept at the Galt House, a splendid hotel, and were handsomely lodged as though we had been in Paris rather than hundreds of miles beyond the Alleghanies." [12]

The remodeled first Galt House is suggestive of the developing Renaissance Revival, with the addition of a story of arched windows and a segmental pediment in the center of the cornice. (*Figure 5*) During the same period the Louisville Hotel, undoubtedly in competition with the Galt House, hired Rogers and Whitestone to enlarge their hotel. The original Louisville Hotel had been completed in 1834. It was designed by Hugh Rowland (Roland) in a hybrid Greek Revival style with shops under a colonnade of ten colossal Ionic columns. The plan was not unlike the Tremont House with large public rooms across the front.

(5) The first Galt House after 1853 remodeling, burned 1865. Demolished. *The Filson Club, Louisville, KY*

Apparently, once the basic formula for a successful hotel had been implemented by Rogers, he used it with modifications for the needs of the site and the city. The new version of the mid-1850s, had 220 rooms in addition to an elaborate office, dining room, ladies' parlor, and reception room, as well as gentlemen's rooms. A central courtyard had a covered passage leading to the water closets. The facade was symmetrical with five stories in a restrained Renaissance Revival mode highlighted by two colossal Corinthian columns at the entrance.[13] (*Figure 6*)

(6) The Louisville Hotel, Louisville, KY. Demolished. The Courier-Journal, 22 December 1944

35

Whitestone's major contribution to hotel design in Louisville was the second Galt House. Rogers and Whitestone's partnership had broken up by 1858. In 1865, the first Galt House burned, Whitestone was chosen to design a new hotel one block east of the original location. The new limestone structure recalled features of the Farnese Palace (1513–40) in Rome. The impetus to use the Farnese Palace as a model probably came from the work of Sir Charles Barry, such as the Traveler's Club and the Reform Club, which Whitestone had already emulated in his residential designs.[14] (*Figure 7*)

Although no plans survive for the second Galt House, fortunately there is a very detailed newspaper account published immediately prior to the opening of the second Galt House in April of 1869. Part of the furniture and decorations is as follows:

The ladies' reception room on the second floor has Wilton carpet, Turkish sofas, and easy chairs, covered with red plush. Large walnut frame mirrors, with cornices to match, and window drapery of heavy rep curtains over lace.[15] (*Figure 8*)

Furnishings came from many sources including washing machines from the Shaker Society in New Hampshire, and carpets, curtain goods, and linens from A. T. Stewart.[16]

This was the only building on which Whitestone allowed his name to be placed. It was a brass plate in the Gentleman's Saloon. A contemporary newspaper article stated that, "The perfection of every detail in the immense hotel having been contributed and superintended by Mr. Whitestone.... The hotel is the immortalizer of the architect."[17]

The plan for the second Galt House, although much larger and more sophisticated mechanically, was not unlike the basic plan for the Tremont House or the Louisville Hotel, in that it contained long hallways running parallel to the front of the building and perpendicular into the wings. In all three structures, the public restrooms or parlors were across the front of the building and there were courtyards within the plan.

The influence of the American hotel was apparently far-reaching and extended beyond the United States. For example, plans by J. Giles for the Langham Hotel, Portland Place, London, published in *The Builder* (London) in 1863, are strikingly similar to Rogers and Whitestone's hotel plans with public rooms across the front, the cross-axial hallways and an interior courtyard.[18] In turn, it is possible that some of the lavish appointments at the Galt House were inspired by the British Clubs.

Not everyone looked with favor upon the large hotels. In 1864, an author in *Duffy's Hibernian Magazine* (Dublin), commented that the word "hotel" was un-

(7)   The second Galt House. Demolished.   Louisville Illustrated, *Louisville*, 1889

English and snobbish, and suggestive of paint and pierglass, of impudent servants and long bills, of discomfort and extortion of indigestion and misery.[19] He said it brought to mind

... those vast places of marble in Philadelphia, and Boston, and New York, with accomodations for two thousand lodgers, with reception rooms, and lavatories, and smoking-rooms, and drawing-rooms, and cloak-rooms, and audience-rooms, and the deuce knows what else with clerks and barbers; with statues and pictures by the old masters; the landlord of which is a colonel in the United States Army, a scholar, and a gentleman; where you can ruin yourself at billiards rouge-et-noir; where you may live a miserable human item of some 1500 eating, drinking, swearing, spitting, tobacco smoking and tobacco chewing citizens of the free and enlightened United States, for some four dollars per day.[20]

The writer preferred the eighteenth-century inn but it is interesting that the formula for large hotels was so similar in 1864, that he could have been describing the yet to be built second Galt House.

Louisville began to turn its back on the Ohio River at the turn-of-the-century, thus, the hotel and retail center moved south away from Main Street. The Galt House declined and in 1921, the Victorian walnut bedsteads were placed in the middle of Main Street for auction. The second Galt House was demolished fifty years after its acclaimed opening.

Whitestone's great work was the second Galt House, however, he was also known for his residential and commercial work, some of which survives.

The American hotel as initially conceived by Isaiah Rogers and executed by Rogers and Whitestone and many others is a phenomenon which has prospered since its origin. Rogers began a trend which earned him the title of "Father of the American Hotel."

(8)   A parlor at the second Galt House.   *The Filson
Club, Louisville, KY*

NOTES

[1] Denys P. Myers, "Isaiah Rogers in Cincinnati," *Historical and Philosophical Society of Ohio Bulletin*, IX (1951), 121–32; Talbot Hamlin, *Greek Revival Architecture in America* (New York: Oxford University Press, 1944), pp. 111–12, 247; Henry F. Withey and E.R. Withey. *Biographical Dictionary of American Architects* (Los Angeles: New Age Publishing Co., ca. 1956), p. 522.

[2] W. H. Eliot, *A Description of the Tremont House* (Boston: Gray and Bowen, 1830).

[3] *Ibid.* Preface.

[4] *Ibid.*, p. 1.

[5] *Ibid.*, p. 3.

[6] Elizabeth F. Jones, "Henry Whitestone: Nineteenth Century Louisville Architect," Unpublished Master's Thesis, University of Louisville (KY.), Department of Fine Arts, 1974; Diary of Augustus Whitestone, Morton Collection, Louisville, Kentucky.

[7] *The Builder*, VIII, 387 (6 July 1850), p. 316.

[8] Letter from Crofton Vandeleur, Kilrush House, West Clare, Dublin, to Abbot Lawrence, December 8, 1852, Morton Collection, Louisville, Kentucky.

[9] Transcript of Isaiah Rogers's Diaries, 14 July 1852, V. 8, p. 853. Columbia University Avery Architectural and Fine Arts Library.

[10] Jones, *Op. Cit.*

[11] Roger Hale Newton, *Town and Davis Architects* (New York: Columbia University Press, 1942), p. 127.

[12] Charles Dickens, *American Notes* (London, 1842), p. 100.

[13] Architectural Drawings for the Louisville Hotel, The Filson Club, Louisville, Kentucky.

[14] Jones, *Op. Cit.*

[15] *The Courier-Journal* (Louisville, Kentucky), 21–22 March 1869.

[16] *Ibid.*

[17] *Ibid.*

[18] J. Mordaunt Crook, *Victorian Architecture: A Visual Anthology* (New York: Johnson Reprint Corp., 1971), p. 182.

[19] *Duffy's Hibernian Magazine*, "Melbourne Hotels," V. (May 1864), p. 333.

[20] *Ibid.*

HEALTH RESTORING RESORTS ON THE NEW ENGLAND COAST

Marie L. Ahearn

NAHANT HOTEL.

HEALTH RESTORING RESORTS ON THE
NEW ENGLAND COAST

Marie L. Ahearn

FRESH AIR OR HEALTHFUL WATER— and sometimes the two in combination—supported the therapeutic health claims made by the nineteenth century resort. Hotels in the mountains and the seaside asserted that the special quality of their air restored health, while inland resorts affirmed the efficacy of pure country and temperate air. At the same time, spas and springs as well as lake and ocean resorts insisted upon the salubrious effects of their local water, either taken internally or externally by immersion. To take the waters and/or breathe the air at such favored sites, it was argued, fostered good health and promoted total physical and mental well being.

Even though mineral springs achieved fame as watering places for the fashionable and wealthy during the nineteenth century, in fact their health claims often were quickly superseded by the glitter of fashion and high society as the true attraction. The fame of Saratoga Springs, for example, was built upon the social scene and horse racing as much as on the efficacy of its mineral water. In competition with the inland spas of the nineteenth century, seaside resorts slowly but steadily increased in popularity as they emphasized the healthful qualities of their sea air and salt water. While most ocean resorts pointed to the wholesomeness of their climate during the hot summer, some were especially insistent upon the benefits in good health to be obtained from a vacation spent in their special ambience.

Nahant, a tiny peninsula on Boston's north shore, was one of the earliest ocean resorts to emphasize summer breezes and salt air as curatives for the invalid and

convalescent. No less an authority than Dr. Walter Channing, Dean of the Harvard Medical School, had said that Nahant's cool summers, equable temperature, "pure, fresh, exhilirating" ocean breezes, and fine opportunities for sea bathing were most desirable for those in poor health. Facts were insufficient, he said, to declare exactly what diseases would be cured by a summer at Nahant, yet he was sure that a visit would benefit weaning children, dyspeptic adults, and the debilitated and emaciated. Channing called for a hotel to be built at Nahant so that appropriate accommodations would be more plentiful.[1] Conveniently enough, Mrs. Channing's uncle, the wealthy merchant Thomas Handasyd Perkins, immediately set about building the Nahant Hotel, which opened for business in 1823.[2]

From the wraparound wooden piazzas of the Nahant Hotel's stone building the visitor could breathe intoxicating quantities of calm or breezy salt air while enjoying a 360° vista of ocean, sand, rocks, or sun. (Figure 1) Similar deep and expansive porches would be prototypical of all future seaside hotels, but with one difference: the Nahant Hotel reserved the first floor piazza for the men, and the second floor for the ladies. While the more sedentary guests could sit on the porches and inhale the salt air, the vigorous could take the air while driving or promenading along the beach and in the grounds adjoining the hotel. In addition, there was a bath house for bathing both indoors and out, in either warm or cold water, salt or plain. The establishment made much of its accommodations: over seventy clean, commodious chambers, various public rooms, and a stone billiard room done in the style of a Greek temple and attached to the main building. The amenities of this fine hotel set amid Nahant's bracing salt air and water in combination with a regimen of gentle diversion could not help but promote health benefits for all—from the invalid and convalescent to

---

(1) Nahant Hotel, 1822-23. Nahant, Mass. *Illustration taken from Caleb Snow. A History of Boston, 1825*

(2) Nahant House, 1828-29. Nahant, Mass. *Illustration taken from Bufford lithograph, c. 1855*

the many who wished to maintain physical well being. In June 1823 the Boston newspapers marked the opening of the new hotel and its wide appeal in these words:

In truth, Nahant is the chosen domain of youthful Hygeia, the pleasant summer residence of the invalid and all those who seek enjoyment or require relaxation from the cares of business life, whether they flee from the sultry clime of the South, or the "Stir of the great Babels" of commerce, there they can be at ease and keep cool.[3]

Cornelius Coolidge, a speculator in land and houses on the Nahant peninsula, erected another hotel in 1828–29—the Nahant House.[4] (*Figure 2*) Though larger than the Nahant Hotel, the new resort also emphasized views in all directions from deep porches while boasting the benefits derived from the circulation of salt air flowing through the window of each guest chamber. In increasing numbers Bostonians took the ferry to Nahant for their vacations; and, as a result, in 1831 the old Nahant Hotel added on one hundred rooms and a dining room. This three story addition aroused much comment, and all of it adverse, because a tall, spare box, punctuated by windows—similar to an ungainly three story motel—was simply plunked down beside the original structure. No attempt was made to harmonize facades, join roof lines, or blend shapes gracefully. In fact, George Washington Curtis declared that the addition had all "the naked ugliness of a cotton factory added" to the original hotel building.[5] And so it was, for the shape and the lighting on the roof of the addition were the very same as the cotton mills in nearby Lowell. Seaside resort architecture would always sacrifice aesthetic considerations and solid construction to short term functionalism, and, therefore, a building that produced numerous guest chambers for the brief summer season had to be preferred to any other alternative. Like early cotton machinery, summer vacationers had to be packed into limited and expensive space at a particular site.

But more than architecture changed at Nahant over the years. If we compare the engraving of the Nahant House done in 1855 by Bufford (*Figure 2*) with the illustration of the Nahant Hotel in Snow's 1825 *History of Boston*, (*Figure 1*) we see that the fashionably dressed vacationers of the era of the 1840s and 1850s were clearly more interested in socializing with each other than they were in the healthy outdoor activities of shooting, fishing, sailing, driving, and walking engaged in by the earlier visitors. The presentation of a Nahant vacation in the 1820s was rustic, not social, emphasizing the simple life in the healthy outdoors. A summer spent in the climate of this peninsula located in the bosom of the ocean and surrounded by plentiful salt air and water presented the invalid with "a per-petual inducement to exercise" even as it provided a bracing tonic to the healthy.[6] In the early years, air, water, and outdoor activity received the emphasis. But notwithstanding the appeal to the convalescent, the invalid, and the maintenance of good health, the image of a healthy Nahant vacation soon gave way to that of a social seaside resort, where the foremost function of sea and air would be that of an agreeable summer background for Bostonians of means.

There were other ocean resorts, however, that never succumbed to fashionable society as their main attraction, but instead steadfastly maintained good health as the primary reason for visiting. The Isles of Shoals, a group of seven tiny islands, about nine miles off Portsmouth, New Hampshire had the great advantage, in one expert's opinion, of possessing "more nearly than almost any other inhabited island in the Western Atlantic" an approximation of the "atmospheric conditions found in a ship at sea."[7] Traditionally, a sea voyage was considered to have a tonic effect, and so was especially recommended for those with chest and respiratory diseases, for invalids, and all convalescent. And yet the expense along with the rigors and seasickness attendant upon an ocean voyage often canceled out any healthful benefits. However, a summer spent on the tiny, rocky islands between New Hampshire and Massachusetts could duplicate all the advantages of a sea voyage without any of its negatives. It was true that life on the Shoals was as confined as life on a ship at sea so thoroughly surrounded by water, save for the rocky headlands that replicated the bridge of an ocean going vessel. In one unflattering description, the largest island, Appledore, was said to contain two trees, an elm and a cherry, a potato patch on the only available soil, and a wild life population that consisted of a cow, some sheep and a snake.[8] In such an environment, suffice it to say, there was no hay fever. Once on these small rocks, one was totally and inescapably immersed in fresh salt air; as the doggerel rhyme of the last century put it:

> The Isles of Shoals, the Isles of Shoals,
> Whose virtues poets oft have sung,
> Where man can live on half a lung....[9]

Dr. Bowditch declared the climate of the Shoals in the summer to be one of the finest in the world, much the best on the Atlantic coast because of its geographical position. Islands off the coast of Maine had cold fogs, and islands south of Cape Cod had warm fogs, he said, but the Shoals had no fog. Neither were there sultry nights nor cold winds; the climate was temperate and equable. Dr. Bowditch closed his observation with the paradoxical conclusion that the climate of the Shoals was at one and the same time both soothing and stimulating.[10]

(3) Laighton's Hotel on Appledore, c. 1880. *Isles of Shoals, N. H.*

Nathaniel Hawthorne made a late August–early September visit to the Shoals in 1852, where he passed the time agreeably: fishing, loafing, writing in his notebooks, and, in general, poking about the rocky sea edges of the two largest isles, Appledore and Star, about a half mile apart. Hawthorne gave this description of the hotel—the Appledore House—built in 1848 by Thomas B. Laighton:

Laighton's Hotel—a large building, with a piazza or promenade before, about 120 feet in length, or more. Yes; it must be more. It is a central edifice of upwards of 70 feet, with two wings. At one end of the promenade is a covered verandah, thirty or forty feet square, so situated that the breeze draws across it, from the sea on one side of the island to the sea on the other; and it is the breeziest and comfortablest place in the world, on a hot day. There are two swings beneath it; and here one may sit or walk, while all other mortals are suffering.[11]

Although the original wing buildings were not balanced and were roughly done, in 1880 the Appledore House not only had built a dock for the ferry, but also its three story central building was now flanked on each side by balanced separate buildings as wings; and all three structures were interconnected by an immense first floor piazza providing an extensive, covered promenade. (*Figure 3*) The total effect was impressive. Nevertheless, on the inside the hostelry was reported to have rather primitive amenities.

In 1873 Mr. John Poor of Stickney and Poor's Spices erected the Oceanic Hotel on Star Island. A much more luxurious establishment, the new hotel advertised its superiority to the accommodations on Appledore by virtue of its direct landing for ferry boats, an elevator and superior plumbing. The Oceanic asserted that a week at the Shoals on Star Island was worth a month in the mountains, the key difference being the salt air. Though the new hotel proved popular its life was short, for it was destroyed by fire just after the second season. The Appledore House, too, would burn in 1914. Fire was the great destroyer of all wooden oceanside hotels and very few managed to withstand the danger and survive intact. In order to open the Oceanic in time for the next season two smaller guest houses on Star Island—the Gosport and Atlantic Houses—were pushed together and joined by a frame that had been intended for an addition to the burned structure.[12] Enlargements, additions, and makeshift arrangements—almost always in wood and seemingly held together by frequent coats of paint—became characteristic of ocean resort buildings in the nineteenth century as hotels struggled to meet the requirements of vacationers descending in great numbers for a short nine or ten week summer season. But always the thrust of prominence would focus upon spacious porches overlooking the ocean with ample room to promenade or sit in numerus sturdy rocking chairs.

The primitive simplicity of a sojourn spent amid nothing but salt air, ocean, and sky promoted physical well being, yet the Shoals also boasted a literary flavor to provide a cultural balm to the mind and spirit—the nurturance of mental health, as it were, to match glowing physical health. The culture of the Shoals centered upon the daughter of Thomas Laighton, Mrs. Celia Thaxter, a celebrated poet of the nineteenth century. To the Victorians her life was the stuff of romance: Celia grew up in the lonely confines of the lighthouse on miniscule White Island tended by the Laighton family and then moved to Appledore where her father and brothers built the hotel. From the age of four her life had been passed within the confines of these lonely isles, so sparse in population, yet resplendent with a harsh and rocky beauty. Celia Laighton married her

(4) Southeasterly parlor in Celia Thaxter's cottage, Appledore. *Isles of Shoals, N. H.*

tutor, young Levi Lincoln Thaxter, a Harvard graduate and devotee of Robert Browning's poetry, who later became partner to her family in the hotel venture. The Shoals and Celia Thaxter proved to be the attraction that drew John Greenleaf Whittier to the isles every summer, as well as the painters William Morris Hunt and Childe Hassam, and Professor John Paine, pianist and composer, who often played for the visitors.[13] Celia's summer literary salon in the setting of her modest cottage became quite celebrated. (*Figure 4*) As proof of her widespread popularity and recognition, her picture appeared on the inside lids of fine cigar boxes; indeed in this honor she joined the famous Lily Langtry and Jenny Lind.

In 1892 Childe Hassam painted Celia Thaxter in "Her Garden," and this became the frontispiece illustration when he collaborated with her on the charming book, *An Island Garden* (1895). Hassam's illustrations were most effective accompaniments to Celia's extended prose narrative about her garden on the rocky isles. She described her preparations and provided her garden plan, discussed fertilizers, bugs and birds, the effective display of flowers, and the annual cycle of nature. She told of her tiny childhood garden on White Island and the larger ones on the ledges of Appledore and Star: "Ever since I could remember anything flowers have been like dear friends to me—comforters, inspirers, powers to uplift and to cheer." When asked the secret of her success with bountiful and blooming flower gardens amid such difficult conditions, Celia said, "I answer with one word, Love." [14] Although noted in her own day as a poet—some poem titles are "The Sunrise Never Failed Us Yet," and "Back from Life's Coasts the Ebbing Tide Has Drawn"—today's reader probably would find more enjoyment in her prose works, *An Island Garden* and *Among the Isles of Shoals*, sketches of life on the isles.[15]

Notwithstanding the formidable attractions of the Isles of Shoals to the thick-soled shoe set of vacationers in search of good health and well being rather than mere fashion, other ocean resorts offered competition. Of these, Block Island, Rhode Island was the most serious contender. The promotional literature for Block Island declared it to be similar to the Shoals in every way yet superior because there were no mosquitoes or biting flies on a larger island possessing a wider selection of accommodations and offering a variety of carriage drives as well as numerous safe bathing beaches

44

of fine sand and warm water. Therefore to spend a summer at sea amid a most pleasantly cool climate, the best choice was Block Island.

Brochures advertising the Ocean View Hotel declared the island to be the paradise of invalids, a haven of rest and recuperation for the weary in body and brain. It was emphasized that this island seven miles long and three miles wide, located ten miles south of the Rhode Island shore and fourteen miles east of Montauk Point, Long Island was not situated upon the coast, "where the unhealthy land breezes counteract the salutary influences of the ocean"; on the contrary, Block Island "stands out boldly in the pure untainted air of the Atlantic." Visitors' testimony was cited to prove the "invigorating and tonic effect of the atmosphere, stimulating appetites and promoting digestion to a wonderful degree." The peculiar tonic of this air, the testimonials solemnly explained, was due to the presence of "ozone and various sea salts" to a much greater degree than exists in the atmosphere of the usual seashore setting.[16] Indeed, the Ocean View Hotel asserted that the oceanic climate of the Block was absolutely pure and, therefore, not the climate of a shore resort where the atmosphere was affected by mainland "malarial swamps, fish factories, and mosquitoes."[17] Obviously these unkind remarks were aimed at the summer competition—Newport and the hotels along the Rhode Island shore. Visitors were assured that whichever way the wind might blow—and on the Block it surely does blow—the breezes would come directly from the ocean, pure and uncontaminated, "so that its effect is truly magical."[18] Indeed, today's visitor so accustomed to the pollution of cities is often overwhelmed by both the enormous quantity and quality of island air.

For many years brochures advertising the island reprinted the testimony of medical doctors to support the health claims of Block Island. Also, in a more personal and psychological advertising ploy, the brochures generally contained some variation upon the following dialogue between prospective summer vacationers:

Where are you going this summer?

Well, I don't know, replied the Judge. I have a large family, and it is difficult to find any one place which will suit us all. My wife has a bad throat and catarrh; one of my daughters has been badly poisoned with malaria, another has nervous prostration from over study, and so on through the whole family. Our physician is trying to persuade us to go to Block Island this year.

Indeed? I am glad to hear this, for we have spent several delightful summers there, and I shall be happy to tell you all about the place.

Needless to say the Judge gets an earful about the healthful qualities of a vacation on Block Island, as he is assured that the "wisest and most sensible health seekers" will choose a watering place not by the crite-

rion of fashion, but by the "strongest claims to health and comfort."[19]

The Ocean View Hotel in the town of New Shoreham at Old Harbor had accommodations for five hundred guests. Facing the ocean on three sides, set high on a bluff, and with a harbor frontage of three hundred and fifty feet nearly every room had a splendid water view. The hotel boasted a grand veranda, twenty feet wide, and a quarter mile in length, looking down on the ocean over fifty feet below. Anyone taking his daily constitutional on this veranda need not worry about hay fever because there was no irritating dust on the island and no "obnoxious vegetable effluvia." The hotel emphasized its hot sea baths, recommended for invalids and the delicate in health in preference to a cold plunge in the ocean. Hot salt baths, it was solemnly avowed, were "never followed by depressing reaction, and are an exceedingly stimulating tonic."[20] From different locations on the hotel's veranda there were a variety of nature's views furnishing gentle stimulation to the mind and so alleviating depression. There was the harbor directly in front, so picturesque with its scores of fishing and pleasure boats; the great breakwater extending out into the ocean to the right; to the westwards alternating green hills and valleys whose placid appearance was punctuated by crystal lakes and ponds, and, far in the distance, on one side the beautiful scenery of the distant mainland across the sound, or, on the other, the sublime expanse of Atlantic Ocean stretching away unbroken. The Ocean View Hotel declared Block Island to be the Bermuda of the North where truly one could spend a summer far out to sea.

Taking its name from the ancient Greek goddess of health, the Hygeia Hotel was built by a physician, Dr. Charles H. Hadley, and so specialized in accommodations for health and comfort. (Figure 5) Situated in New Harbor—reached from Old Harbor and New Shoreham by free horse trolley—on an elevated knoll between two small lakes and with an ocean overlook, the Hygeia had large, airy rooms, each with an open fireplace, wash bowl, and running spring water. It also boasted fine opportunities for bathing: hot and cold sea water and shower baths inside as well as surf bathing near at hand. (Figure 6) The Hygeia repeatedly noted that there was no malaria on the island because it was never stifling hot, and, moreover, the freedom from dust, noise, and excitement contributed to a restful atmosphere. But in case of a health emergency a physician was in attendance.[21]

Reflecting a less elaborate version of the style of wooden domestic architecture to be found in Newport and vicinity in the 1870s—the stick style of Dudley Newton's Sturtevant (Jacob Cram) house in Middle-

Block Island, R. I. - Hygeia Hotel

(7) New Hygeia Hotel, c. 1899. Horse trolley to Old Harbor. *Block Island, R. I.*

town, R. I., for example[22]—the Hygeia's block shape was made fragile by the light verticality of the slender timbers of the porches, the tall and narrow windows, and the sharply angled gables held down by the square, but rising tower; the whole effect was that of a light, airy, summery cottage. Business was good at the Hygeia so that in 1899 the building was enlarged to become the New Hygeia. (*Figure 7*) To create the larger building, the original structure was simply built out at the sides with verandas leading the way. In the transformation the gables and tower receded in their central prominence as their verticality gave way to the horizontal solidity of the extending wings. Thus the Hygeia became solid and prosperous, definitely a hotel, an institution that could not now be mistaken for a summer family cottage.

_____

(5) Old Hygeia Hotel, c. 1886. *Block Island, R. I.*

(6) Hot and cold sea water and shower baths. Hygeia Hotel. *Block Island, R. I.*

All the hotels on the Block repeatedly mentioned their pure drinking water and fine drainage. The pure air, cool nights, salt baths, and temperate climate in combination with sanitary and hygienic conditions that were near perfect, it was avowed, created circumstances unrivaled for good health. Besides these favorable attributes, there was also immeasurable benefit to be gained from the calm tenor of island life, the unsurpassed opportunities for moderate exercise in the fresh air and salt water, and the wholesome diet of island vegetables and fresh fish. Certainly physical well being followed from this array of positive influences, and, therefore, a summer of island life would bring relief from a broad range of illnesses: asthma, dyspepsia, fatigue, anemia, overworked brains, pthistical sufferers of night sweats, as well as certain eye diseases. Block Island was good for what ailed you!

Unable to compete with the wealth of Newport and the fashion of other Long Island and Rhode Island shore resorts, the Block sought out its own summer visitor: the respectable member of the middle class. Smaller guest houses and cottages abounded on the island, almost all with a decidedly Victorian flavor. Prospective vacationers were assured that their fellow visitors would be "solid men and women of the most moral circles of the country"; people who sought health and temperate pleasure, and cared less for the "gaudy shows of the fashionable resorts than for the pleasures of Nature's walks" in the out-of-doors.[23] The appeal to middle class Victorian psychology was marvelously maintained in the invocation of Ben Franklin's axiom, "Health is Wealth." Thus the middle class father or working man or woman was assured that a Block Island vacation would be no mere frivolous expenditure or wasted time; on the contrary it was an investment in good health. Although vacation time might be leisure time the days spent on this island were never wasted because they were an effective means of building up or maintaining good health, without which worldly business could not be properly conducted. Because a Block Island vacation had this most important use and purpose the middle class upholder of the Protestant Ethic need not feel guilty about taking time away from work; after all a vacation for health was not frivolous. It was a wise man who heeded the wisdom of the old saying: "Better to hunt in fields for health unbought,/Than fee the doctor for a nauseous draught."

Unfortunately the Block could not match the Shoals and Celia Thaxter in genteel culture, and so had to fall back on history and legend for sentiment and improvement. Shipwrecks formed the only subject matter of the island's romantic past. Fortunately that peripatetic summer vacationer, John Greenleaf Whittier wrote a poem about one of the island disasters—the wreck of the Palatine. Although circumstances surrounding this shipwreck remained mysterious, it became the custom for the summer visitor to view the site of the wreck at Sandy Point on the island's northern tip, lament the sad fate of the ship's passengers, and recite some lines from Whittier's stirring description of the sea girt isle. And in the poem Whittier characterized Block Island as a place where "...the pale health-seeker findeth there/The wine of life in its pleasant air." [24]

NOTES

[1] Walter Channing, M.D., *A Topographic Sketch of Nahant*, with comparative meteorological tables for July, August, and September, 1820, with some observations on its advantages as a watering place (1821), *passim* pp. 1–7. This pamphlet is a reprint of Channing's article in the *New England Journal of Medicine and Surgery* (January 1821).

[2] Joseph E. Garland, *Boston's North Shore Being an Account of Life Among the Noteworthy, Fashionable, Wealthy, Eccentric and Ordinary 1823–90* (Boston: Little, Brown, 1978), pp. 31–35. See also, Rebecca M. Rogers, "Resort Architecture at Nahant 1815–1850," *SPNEA Bulletin* Vol. LXV Nos. 1–2 (Summer-

Fall 1974), 17–19. For Nahant, see also, Alonzo Lewis and James R. Newhall, *History of Lynn* (Boston, 1829); and Alonzo Lewis, *The Picture of Nahant* (Lynn: J. B. Tolman, 1848).

[3] Fred A. Wilson, *Some Annals of Nahant Massachusetts* (Nahant Historical Society, reprinted 1977), p. 77.

[4] Rogers, pp. 19–25; Wilson, Chapter VI "Hotels," pp. 72–91.

[5] George Washington Curtis, *Lotus Eating: A Summer Book* (New York: Harper and Bros., 1852), p. 145.

[6] Channing, p. 5.

[7] S. G. W. Benjamin, *The Atlantic Islands as Resorts of Health and Pleasure* (New York: Harper and Co., 1878), p. 272. See also David Francis Lincoln, M.D., "Notes on the Climate of the Isles of Shoals, and of Nantucket" (Boston: H. O. Houghton, 1875), reprinted from the *Boston Medical and Surgical Journal* (October 1875).

[8] William M. Varrell, *Summer by-the-sea* (Portsmouth, N. H.: Strawberry Bank, 1972), p. 96.

[9] *Ibid.*, p. 16.

[10] Frank Preston Stearns, *Sketches from Concord & Appledore* (New York: G. P. Putnam Sons, 1895), pp. 251–52.

[11] Nathaniel Hawthorne, *The American Notebooks*, ed. Claude M. Simpson, Vol. VIII (Ohio State Univ.: Centenary Edition, 1972), p. 512.

[12] Lyman V. Rutledge, *Ten Miles Out Guide Book to the Isles of Shoals* (Boston, Isles of Shoals Assoc., 1972), p. 9.

[13] Stearns, *Sketches*, see the Chapter, "Appledore and the Laightons."

[14] Celia Thaxter, *An Island Garden* with Pictures and Illuminations by Childe Hassam (Boston: Houghton Mifflin Co., 1895), Prefatory, p. V, and p. 5.

[15] Celia Thaxter, *Among the Isles of Shoals* (Boston: J. R. Osgood and Company, 1878). There were numerous editions of her poems, for example, *Poems* (New York: Hurd and Houghton, 1874 and 1875).

[16] *Ocean View Hotel*, Block Island, Rhode Island (Boston: Deland & Barta, 1882), descriptive circular. C. E. Brown, *The Manisses* (Hotel), Block Island (Boston: Deland & Barta, n.d.).

[17] "Block Island as a Health Resort," by H. Holbrook Curtis, M.D., in *Block Island, A Summer at Sea* (Providence: C. E. Littlefield, n.d.), pp. 14–15.

[18] *Ocean View Hotel* (1882), p. 11.

[19] *A Summer at Block Island*, Manisses Hotel (Boston: Deland & Barta, 1886), pp. 1–2.

[20] *Ocean View Hotel* (1882), p. 16.

[21] *The New Hygeia*, Block Island, Rhode Island, pamphlet, n.d.

[22] See Vincent J. Scully, Jr., *The Shingle Style and The Stick Style*, revised edition (New Haven: Yale Univ. Press, 1971), pp. lvi–lvii.

[23] Rev. S. T. Livermore, *A History of Block Island* (Hartford, Conn.: Lockwood & Brainard Co., 1877), pp. 228–29. See also Ben Mush, *Block Island: A Handbook, with Map* (Norwich, Conn.: James Hall, 1877).

[24] John Greenleaf Whittier, *Complete Poetical Works* (Boston: Houghton Mifflin, 1894), pp. 258–59.

ON THE VERANDAH:
RESORTS OF THE CATSKILLS

Betsy Blackmar and Elizabeth Cromley

ON THE VERANDAH:
RESORTS OF THE CATSKILLS

Betsy Blackmar and Elizabeth Cromley

FOR 160 YEARS the Catskill Mountains in New York State have served the changing needs of urban Americans seeking a nearby vacation paradise.[1] Resort owners and resort-goers have transformed what was a hunting and agricultural landscape into an intensely developed tourist mecca. In 1823, the Catskill Mountain House stood alone as a specialized tourist hotel; by the 1880s, resort hotels and boarding houses in the Catskills accommodated over 70,000 guests every summer.

The Catskill area is a three-thousand square mile, four county region around the Catskill and Shawangunk mountain ranges. Greene and Delaware counties comprise the northern section of the region, Ulster and Sullivan counties the southern. The quality of these landscapes is noticeably different from north to south. Nature is rugged in the northern (or "true") Catskills with abrupt notches between mountains, rushing streams and numerous waterfalls—small, yet breathtaking. This is the landscape where Romantic Hudson River School painters found an uncultivated Eden for their canvases of the 1840s and 1850s. In the south, the Shawangunk range has some equally attractive scenery, but it is less imposing in scale; as one moves west, a lovely undulant landscape replaces mountain peaks with meadows.

Visitors began going up the Hudson to the mountains by sailboat and steamship as early as the 1820s. In the 1870s, the Ulster and Delaware Railroad following the Hudson River, and the New York Ontario and Western Railway moving northwest into Sullivan County, made the entire region easily accessible to

thousands of visitors who retreated annually from the stiffling summer air of the New York, New Jersey, and Pennsylvania metropolitan and industrial region.

Accommodations ranged from farm houses that took in summer boarders "as part of the family," to elegant hotels that orchestrated elaborate social seasons for their more wealthy guests. The Victorian era left a legacy of diversity in resort building which is still in place today.

In the face of such diversity in building styles and scales spread over 150 years, an analysis of the Catskill resort may seem doomed from the start. Yet if we look at the resort as a group of ad hoc buildings that, in a sense, collaborate with vacationers to arrive at forms most adapted to their needs, then the external trappings of style take second place to an understanding of the resort buildings as places suited to their tasks. Behind the rustic or classical or carpenter gothic facades, a stable set of functional architectural features have supplied the basic alphabet of Catskill resorts over their long lifetime, and can still be seen today, looking very different but expressing and fulfilling some of the same purposes.

We shall focus our inquiry on the verandah of the resort, the space that, sharing both outdoor and indoor properties, stood at the center of the Victorian resort world.[2] In typical 19th century American usage, visitors often called the big front porch the "piazza," confusing the arcades that surround the typical Italian piazza with the name of the open square itself. (Figure 1) In choosing the name "verandah," we evoke the architectural motif of attached, semi-sheltered, semi-open space that recurs from the Indian bungalow to the southern plantation house. Mediating between inside and outside, the verandah linked the natural setting and the social activity of the resort hotel. It was at the same time a frontispiece, almost a frame for the hotel—the best and most prominent piece of architectural work on

51

(2) Olcott House, Wurtsboro, New York, c. 1870. An elaborate three-level verandah wraps around the street facades. *Collection Manville Wakefield/ Barbara Purcell*

the building—and also a frame for the view from the hotel. Through this frame, guests entered the special social scene of the Catskill "summer home."

The verandah was a defining trait of Victorian resorts. It served as a sign; just as a striped barber pole signifies a barber's shop, so did the verandah advertise the building as a hotel. In towns where other public institutions—the bank, courthouse, or town hall—might have columned porticos, the hotels did not stop at an accentuated entry, but expanded the verandah the full length of the building, even to two or three sides, and to second and third stories. (*Figure 2*) Seeing this distinctive hotel feature, every stranger knew in a moment where to find lodgings. In the mountains, the verandah worked not simply to identify the hotel, but also to beautify it and thus to enhance the ensemble of a-building-in-the-scenery for approaching travelers.

The verandah spoke for the building it fronted, and sometimes even instead of the building. Many Catskill hotels were extremely simple, clapboard boxes with only minimal gestures toward ornament. For these "decorated shed" buildings, the verandah constituted the chief decoration, the only especially architectural effect. In more elaborate buildings, the verandah often concentrated within itself all the elements of "style" in the building, introducing architectural themes echoed throughout the hotel. One of the most famous Catskill verandahs was also the region's first: the magnificent carved corinthian columns that fronted the Catskill Mountain House presented Greek revival motifs repeated by cornices, interior woodwork, and interior columns. (*Figure 3*) The columns themselves reportedly had been originally intended for the state capitol building. In 1881, Philadelphia architect S. D. Button created the elaborate carved wood verandah of the Hotel Kaaterskill and attempted to carry that grandeur throughout the interior with black walnut panelling and Eastlake furniture.

Proprietors built verandahs on the side of the hotel from which one could take in the best view. For carefully sited hotels, verandahs could embrace the scenery on two or three sides of the hotel buildings, and on occasion they wrapped the entire structure. On the

(3) Catskill Mountain House, perched on its cliff. *Thomas Nast's drawing for* Harper's Weekly Magazine, 21 July 1866

theory that it was impossible to have too much of a good thing, proprietors added to verandah space by means of balconies, or second and third stories, still sheltered by the porch roof. The Hotel Kaaterskill had a center gable with imposing verandah columns reaching up four stories. The side wings featured three story columns, and in the center a second floor balcony offered guests a second point of view. The Grand Hotel's 1881 angled plan allowed a verandah that faced in three directions, one story high on its flanks and two stories in the center. (*Figure 4*) This verandah was a fantasy of jigsaw work with nearly moorish arches, and towers that the proprietors preferred to describe as Queen Ann style. In some hotels the verandah worked as a device for linking and unifying separate parts of the building. Fronted with a stylish verandah, successive additions of an expanding hotel could all be made to match.

More than architectural ornaments, verandahs fulfilled the essential purpose of resort hotels by bringing the guests into contact with nature. Just as eighteenth century Grand Tourists viewed nature through a Claude glass, so Catskill visitors received the prospect of the mountains and valleys as carefully column-framed wonders. Without being overly manipulative, the verandah directed the guests toward a likely focus, suggesting that the best view only exists for the correctly placed viewer. With standard verandah equipment—sketchbook and binoculars followed by the first Kodaks—guests confirmed the judgment of the hotels' architects who aligned the buildings with the best of the natural landscape.

The verandah's situation—partly sheltered, partly outdoors—allowed guests to partake of the benefits of outdoor life without fully exposing themselves to nature.

The verandah thus became the place to enhance health by brisk walks after dinner, to recuperate from forays into the mountains, and to take the air in inclement weather. In the days when fresh air was a serious goal for guests fleeing congested cities, the verandah was as important to the summer's regimen as pools and tennis courts are today. Guests compared laps taken up and down the verandah as joggers would compare miles, and the hotel with the longest was clearly the best. In the 1890s Churchill Hall proudly advertised 650 feet of continuous verandah!

Guests could pursue nature even more intimately in the Catskill gazebo or summer house which was a common offshoot of the verandah. Standing on the lawn as if a little independent fragment of the parent porch, or dotting mountain trails, the gazebo offered privacy to two or three visitors where the verandah entertained a whole crowd. Sometimes these gazebos repeated the same style as the verandah, as with the gazebo at Thompson House, and sometimes they developed their own independent rustic style, as in the bark gazebos at Mohonk.

We have approached the verandah first as a physical artifact. But just as importantly, the verandah provided a social focal point for Victorian hotels, the place where guests could encounter, observe and judge first nature and then one another.

With its southern and domestic overtones, the verandah symbolized the hospitality and reception of the private home, the summer home. The rocking chairs and porch rails, healthy breezes and adjacent lawn conjured up the serenity and the safety of the extended and watchful family and neighborhood. As such the verandah represented the social domain of a particular group in Victorian society, the middle class who could afford single family houses with porches and lawns (rather than stoops and streets), and who could afford summer vacations. Within that class, the home was the particular domain of a second class, of women. As Andrew Jackson Downing, Catharine Beecher and others attached an ideology of family, health and nurture to the private, suburban home in the second half of the 19th century, so too did promoters of summer homes and resorts stress the virtues of a homelike retreat from the city.[3] Yet the verandah also sheltered contradictions that stood at the heart of Victorian resort life: these summer homes were *not* private, guests on the verandah did *not* necessarily know and trust one another, and the hospitality of the hotel carried with it both the opportunity for public contact and the risks of public exposure. In the eyes of many observers, the verandah was the emblem not of the home as haven but of the competition for recognition and status that

(4) Grand Hotel, Catskill, New York, 1881. *Private Collection*

seemed so much a part of "new" urban society.[4] To reflect on the verandah's social life, then, is to reflect on further tensions underlying middle class Victorian society.

Guests at Catskill hotels often returned year after year to the same resort or boarding house. Women came for the season, from six to ten weeks, while husbands and fathers usually came by train for weekends. By virtue of a summer's stay, women established their own communities, both within the individual hotels and among neighboring hotels in resort towns such as Liberty, Haines Falls, and Fleischmanns. (*Figure 5*) Before the advent of intensely programmed daily activities after the turn of the century, most of the entertainment at the numerous modest Catskill boarding houses echoed the daily rhythms of genteel family life —meals, trips to the drugstore and postoffice, correspondences, and lawn sports, with the verandah at the crossroads of all comings and goings.

In 1884, Annie Searing described the scene:

Coming out of the dining room, a burst of sunshine on the verandah caused universal rejoicing. There was a rush for hats and walking sticks . . . troops of laughing girls and a few dapper youth went to the tennis ground, the children to the swings and croquet while the stout dowagers took possession of the verandah.[5]

The image of the verandah as the special territory of women also made it a favored object of ridicule for satirists who scoffed at the "gossips" who seemed to dominate the porch and from there the entire resort

community. In 1893, one journalist typically reported of the hotel season: "One element is here that will be found at every summer resort in the country. She is the gossip. As a rule she is old and not prepossessing. She sits about the hotel verandah all the time and criticizes her neighbors." [6] Yet life on the verandah for Victorian women was not the utterly idle and carefree affair projected by still photographs and literary images of gossips. In exchange for the responsibility of maintaining the private household, women at summer homes assumed a new set of obligations, that of supervising their own and their family's public interactions. (*Figure 6*)

As a public sphere, the resort required attention to presentation. The informality of resort activity and resort fashions merely disguised the never-absent formality of public encounters. The verandah served as the proscenium of a stage.[7] Viewed kindly, the "play" was recreation. But for many summer guests in the Catskills the play carried a particular urgency of confirming or maintaining social status.

The ideology that expected Victorian middle class women to find their fulfillment in the home presented a basic dilemma when it came time for members of that class to establish new homes. How were they to meet suitable mates? For the upper classes, the city social season served this basic function of introducing the children of elite families to eligible prospects. But for those women who could not afford the lavish social circuit of the leisure class, and for the young men whose work schedules did not leave much free time for socializing, and for the families of both, introducing young people became a source of legitimate concern. The summer season allowed the private family to go public, to

(5)   **Winter Clove, Purling, New York, in 1878.**
Collection Mert Whitcomb

expand, as it were, their pool of opportunity. Thus social reformer James Ford described a classic resort figure,

The woman with two marriageable daughters who weigh heavily on her mind is always hunting for . . . some place where there is 'something going on,' as she would express it, signifying the opportunity for them to make desirable acquaintances and perhaps encounter some eligible young men who would make good husbands for the maidens in question.[8]

The Victorian resort assumed a special function as the theater of courtship. The verandah with its protected space offered the perfect setting for the rituals of courtship. It allowed the shopping around that matched a society committed to the free market but reluctant to let that market into its private sphere.

Courtship involved more than individuals exploring their mutual interests and opportunities. Courtship was a principle medium for the social mobility—the "climbing"—that disturbed many outside observers of resort life and that contradicted the versions of summer homes as insulated genteel retreats. The masquerades, a favored resort passtime, accentuated the manipulations, disguise and mistrust that added a peculiar tension to summerhome life. Where social "opportunity" introduced a new element of risk to resort life, the verandah supplied a comfortable and unobtrusive base from which to keep tabs on the field of social intercourse and exchange. The women who observed and commented on other guests were surveilling those people with whom they suddenly shared both a summer home and the prospect of a family future.

Given guests' ever-present consciousness of other guests, the hotels themselves undertook to reassure their clientele by exercising the most obvious modes of restriction and control over the composition of summer homes. The Catskill landscape is remarkable for the diversity of its hotels, but the main difference among hotels and boarding houses in the Victorian era was the economic position of the people who frequented them. The grand hotels of the railroad era—the Kaaterskill,

55

(6)   Most summer boarders were women, as seen on this unidentified 19th century verandah.   *Collection Manville Wakefield/Barbara Purcell*

the Grand, Churchill Hall or Mohonk—guaranteed a certain "respectability" among their guests simply by being expensive. Desiring yet more control, some of the large hotels filtered their clientele by requiring references and deliberately cultivating their own genteel and gentile reputations. Mohonk, for example, presented itself as a sober and refined setting—"at once a resort, a home, and a church"—and sought to discourage visitors interested in a frivolous or an aggressive social life.

For the hundreds of boarding houses and more modest hotels that sprang up in the Catskills in the 1880s, the protective screen of cost did not work; and boarding house guests felt themselves vulnerable to the uncertainties of unrestricted public encounters. This vulnerability may help account for the extreme hostility with which Catskill boarding houses met visitors who did not fit into the "old American," gentile resort community. Currents of nativism and antisemitism ran through Victorian hotels from Saratoga to the Jersey shore in the 1880s, but the sustained exclusionary policies of the Catskill boarding houses attested to the particular anxiety of their guests. In a typical notice, one hotel explained,

People not familiar with Catskills, know that except at the large hotels, Jews and Gentiles will not generally board at the same house. This is to be regretted, but being the fact, the houses have to take one class or the other. Therefore, the proprietor begs to say that the Loxhurst accommodates gentiles only.[9]

The fabric of nativism is complex; but newly successful immigrant groups, particularly German Jews, did not fit into the Victorian, gentile and family-centered culture of boarding house life.[10] Later immigrant guests,

particularly eastern European Jews, differed by class as well as by ethnic background. For women charged with the responsibility of guarding their culture, the logical outcome of surveillance was exclusion.

Successful immigrants responded by establishing their own separate resorts in the Catskills, recreating in the mountains the ethnic neighborhoods of the cities, and creating, in effect, their own verandahs where they too could go home again. Within their ethnic clusterings, resort-goers could regain their confidence that other guests shared enough of the same cultural background values and economic status to share a life as well. The history of resort prejudice and ethnic exclusion becomes most difficult to analyze when perceived as a strategy to preserve cultural integrity as well as social status for different social, ethnic and religious groups. The lively description of a Jewish Catskill resort in Abraham Cahan's 1917 novel *The Rise of David Levinsky* suggests that the social life itself continued much as it had in gentile hotels.

Thus the diversity of the Catskill resorts went beyond the buildings to include the composition of guests whose new needs shaped the architecture to come. By the end of the nineteenth century, the verandah had ceased to dominate the social life of the resort, but this architectural feature remained to take on new forms and new tasks in the twentieth.

One characteristic of Catskill resorts that remains fairly constant is that they were never the right size. In prosperous years they were too small, and in lean years too big. In the lucky years of booming business when more rooms were needed, the verandah proposed itself as potential room. It already had a floor and a ceiling and was attached to the main building—just an enclosing wall and: instant addition. Hotels with hardy guests often put extra cots for them on the verandah, turning it into bedrooms for the night. But for some hotels the temptation was too great, and the verandah's potential was made actual by permanent walls filling in the open sides. Filling in the columns, making a solid container with windows rather than a permeable collonaded container—this was the direction of change in an era where nature was receding as the main focus of a Catskill vacation. As the hotels grew, their parlors and lobbies encroached on verandah space, as at Brown's where a partial verandah still stands as an unused reminder of old times, good for putting down your suitcase while waiting for the car to drive up. Some hotels made more stylish adaptations like the Polonia or the Flagler where a ground floor sun-filled space surrounded by tall arched windows, filled with plants and rattan furniture, preserved some of the verandah's outdoor flavor and views. (*Figure 7*)

(7) New Flagler Hotel, Fallsburg, New York, 1920.
Collection Manville Wakefield/Barbara Purcell

Motel-style additions draw on the verandah's historical function as protected outdoor circulation space. No internal corridors link the rooms; entry to every room is from the verandah. This has the virtue of giving each room a sense of independence, each guest a separate front door; but entrance is no longer a shared public experience as it was on the Victorian verandah.

In recent years the largest Catskill resorts have added verandah-like circulation links between the separate buildings of a complex—but these are almost always glassed-in spaces, designed especially to be proof against the weather and move the guest safely, hair-do intact, from bedroom to night club. Some of these glassed-in corridors are big enough to be parlors at the same time they serve circulation needs: Grossinger's Verandah Room is one such.

The verandah's metamorphosis into forms of modern architecture has been far reaching. So many of its functions have gone. As sign, it has been replaced by the billboard and the parking lot. As ornament, by shiny metal and glass. As frame for the view—why, who looks at nature any more?

Yet the space that the verandah provided—part outdoors, part in—finds an echo in the poolside deck or patio, a modern version significantly turned in on itself. Resort-goers will always be concerned with the social life they create for each other. The sociable, informal, protected yet open zone that vacationers were so fond of in the nineteenth century is still the kind of space people need today.

NOTES

The authors would like to acknowledge the support of the Gallery Association of New York State and the Architectural League of New York who sponsored research leading to the exhibition *Resorts of the Catskills*, currently being circulated to New York State Museums by the Gallery Association.

1 This paper is an exploration of one of the themes in our book *Resorts of the Catskills* (New York: St. Martin's and the Gallery Association of New York State, 1979). The book includes essays by authors Blackmar and Cromley, Alf Evers, Neil Harris; and photographs by John Margolies. An extended bibliographic note will be found there. For basic background on the Catskill region's architecture see: Alf Evers, *The Catskills from Wilderness to Woodstock* (Garden City, NY, 1972); Manville Wakefield, *To the Mountains by Rail* (Grahamsville, NY, 1970); and Roland van Zandt, *The Catskill Mountain House* (New Brunswick, NJ, 1966).

2 For an essay on the hotel in general see Nikolaus Pevsner, *A History of Buildings Types* (Princeton, NJ, 1976), chap. 11.

3 For the cult of domesticity, see Ann Douglas, *The Feminization of American Culture* (New York, 1977) and Kathryn Kish Sklar, *Catharine Beecher: A Study in American Domesticity* (New Haven, 1973).

4 Christopher Lasch, *Haven in a Heartless World* (New York, 1978). Though we find Lasch's formulation of the place of the home in American life provocative, we do not concur in his conclusions.

5 A. E. P. Searing, *The Land of Rip Van Winkle: A Tour Through the Romantic Parts of the Catskill, Its Legends and Tradition* (New York, 1884).

6 For a valuable discussion of the rituals of public life see Richard Sennett, *The Fall of Public Man* (New York, 1977).

7 James Ford, "The Old Fashioned Summer Hotel" *Munsey's Magazine*, Volume 21 (May 1899), p. 478.

9 Ulster and Delaware Railroad Company, *The Catskill Mountains* (Kingston, NY, 1891).

10 Alice Hyneman Rhine, "Race Prejudice at Summer Resorts" *The Forum*, Vol. III (July 1887), pp. 521–31. For a study of nativism in this period see John Higham, *Strangers in the Land: American Nativism 1860–1925* (New York, 1969).

WICKER: THE VACATION FURNITURE

Katherine B. Menz

MAIN ENTRANCE GALEN HALL, ATLANTIC CITY

(2) Entrance halls in hotels were frequently furnished with wicker, thus creating an instant impression of entering an atmosphere of relaxation and ease. *Postcard, Galen Hall, Atlantic City, New Jersey*

(3) Wicker's popular use on ship board inspired this hotel to furnish one of their sitting rooms, in which they desired to present a nautical theme, with wicker chairs, settees, and tables. *Postcard, Colton Manor, Atlantic City, New Jersey*

WICKER: THE VACATION FURNITURE

Katherine B. Menz

URING THE 1850s two prominent authorities on country houses—Andrew Jackson Downing and Gervase Wheeler—agreed in their published works that it was very difficult to find furnishings suitable for the mid-nineteenth century country dwelling. Advised Downing: "A country house ... should always be furnished with more chasteness and simplicity than a town house, because it is in the country, if anywhere we should find essential ease and convenience ..." [1]

Downing continued: "Of course, it is as yet difficult to find such furniture—because most of our patterns are of Parisian taste, designed for town houses." Downing then recommended several appropriate furniture styles. For cottages, he favored the "cheap and light" as he describes it, painted furniture made by Hennessy of Boston and he added that "this furniture is so successful that designs more suitable for large country houses are sure to follow." [2]

In a book published in 1851, one year after Downing's, Wheeler wrote: "A home in the country requires furniture in its way more difficult to select than to choose between this and that costly article ... for town use." [3] Furthermore, Wheeler continued, "it is doubtful whether, as yet, the true ideal has been already reached in country furniture." [4]

Wheeler was not as fond of the painted furniture as Downing. Although he mentions ironwork and enameled ware, Wheeler favored what he called "cane furniture," which was discussed with accompanying illustrations in his chapter on "summer furniture." (Figure 1) He wrote:

A material now in very general use in this country, the rattan or cane of the East Indies, affords, an immense variety of articles of furniture, so strong, light, and inexpensive, that it seems peculiarly adapted to general introduction in rural homes. [5]

When Wheeler and Downing expressed these opinions at mid-century, furniture made of rattan (more generally called wicker) was beginning to become increasingly popular largely due to its suitability for use in summer dwellings and outdoors, on porches and lawns. Its use soon spread to the town dwelling; and it became an important element in domestic furnishings throughout the second half of the nineteenth century, reaching a height of popularity between 1890 and the First World War. By 1900, one furniture company was able to state that "no up-to-date, well furnished house is complete without a few pieces of reed and rattan furniture." [6]

A study of the use of wicker in vacation homes, hotels, excursion trains, boats, health resorts, and the city dwelling shows that a major reason for the great popularity of wicker is its associations with the "country" life of "ease and convenience" as Andrew Jackson Downing described it. The late nineteenth century resort setting from Atlantic City, NJ to Lake Tahoe, California adopted this convenient style and frequently contained large collections of wicker. (Figures 2 and 3)

(1) Gervase Wheeler illustrated rattan furniture made in New York City by the J. & C. Berrian Co. Gervase Wheeler, Rural Homes (New York, 1851), p. 197

By the turn of the century, the frequent appearance of wicker as a background prop in nineteenth century illustrative material such as advertisements and illustrations for novels and short stories emphasizes the nineteenth century association of wicker with the outdoors and leisure time. Wicker was often used where an impression of good health, relaxation or leisure was desired. For example, a Mellin's Baby Food advertisement showed a child standing in a wicker chair with the caption beneath which stated "Mellin's Food ... gives increased vitality and strength, and allows the child to develop naturally."[7] The wicker chair assists in creating the atmosphere of health and strength which the advertisement aimed at conveying.

A favorite scene used in advertisements for household gadgets showed a woman standing or sitting beside a wicker chair to suggest leisure time while written material extolled the virtue of the particular gadget. One example (Figure 4) is a scene found on a trade card for the Household Sewing Machine which portrayed two young women on a veranda holding tennis racquets, one of whom is sitting in a wicker chair. Able to take advantage of extra leisure time, these women were portrayed as enjoying the healthful outdoor life.

The late nineteenth century popular romantic novel also often incorporated a wicker chair or two to help set the stage for the romantic scene. The marriage proposal would take place far away from city and its attendant evils, in the country, outdoors, with hero and heroine in wicker chairs.

For example, in a scene from *Heart's Content*, by the popular nineteenth century novelist Ralph Henry Barbour, the heroine stretches herself at length in the wicker chaise lounge on the porch and betrothed-to-be seats himself beside her "with a deep sigh of satisfaction" and they were fanned by southerly breezes which "yielded spicy perfume."[8]

Wicker was, by the inherent qualities of the material used in its construction, particularly well adapted to become the suitable furnishing for the country dwelling which Downing and Wheeler felt was needed. The cane used in wicker furniture was resilient and comfortable and the open weave of the design allowed for ventilation, making wicker an ideal hot weather furniture and "Especially desirable from a sanitary standpoint" as one author on household furnishings described it.[9] Wicker furniture manufacturers in their catalogues and advertising stressed these advantages with such captions as "especially adapted for use at the seashore, being cool, durable, and elegant"[10] and "cool and comfortable for the summer season."[11] (Figure 5) At the seaside, wicker was used on the beach in a variety of ways from bathing machine to rolling cart (a sort of

(4) Wicker was often used as a background prop in advertising to help create a leisure atmosphere. Courtesy, Henry Francis duPont Winterthur Museum, Joseph Downs Manuscript Collection, No. 71X247.10-11, Box 34, p. 23

(5) Although wicker furniture manufacturing companies advertised wicker year round, special efforts were made prior to the summer season. The Paine Furniture Company claimed this rattan suit was "specially designed for seashore or country cottages." *The Paine Furniture Company, Catalogue, Boston, Massachusetts, 1893*

rickshaw); however, its most popular use was a hooded beach chair which afforded protection from the sun at the same time it allowed healthful seabreezes to reach the lounger. Being lightweight and easily movable was another feature stressed as making wicker particularly suitable for the summer dwelling. *The Decorator and Furnisher*—a popular arbiter of taste—advised: "Rattan furniture has the advantage of lightness, allowing chairs and tables being easily moved in warm weather from apartments to verandas and lawns." [12]

Another article in the same magazine went into greater detail on the suitability of wicker for the veranda, or "fresh air parlor," as it was frequently called. The article said, "The most enjoyable part of every summer home is the broad veranda, and for this nothing can take the place of rattan furniture." [13] Again the magazine commented that rattan was so light a child could move it, "a valuable quality in selecting things for out-door use." [14] At first, wicker porch furniture was intended to be an extension of the indoor summer parlor; however, it was not long before specific pieces of furniture were specially designed by the wicker manufacturers for the porch, such as the lounge with magazine pockets:

The half-reclining chair is a compromise with the lounge which many people prefer and it finds great favor with delicate people and invalids . . . There are also capacious easy chairs, with adjustable backs which can be raised or lowered at will. A capacious pocket or rack of some sort should be provided for newspapers and magazines, as the frolic wind likes to play with these, and soon creates great havoc. [15]

The light and airy qualities of wicker coincided with one of the overall decorative schemes considered ideal during the last quarter of the century for the summer parlor or summer house—the Oriental style. The well-known author Harriet Spofford in her book *Art Decoration Applied to Furniture* (1878) wrote:

It will be confessed that as bright and and gay a surrounding as youth and happiness can desire on summer days will be found in these light and open rooms furnished in the Chinese or the Japanese style. [16]

The chairs which she recommends for these rooms are rattan and bamboo. Not only were the Oriental styles, the Chinese, Japanese and Moorish—as Spofford called them—viewed as light, airy, bright and gay but this setting imparted an air of luxury and ease, and tinge of "the romantic" by virtue of being exotic. The author of a book entitled *House and Home* wrote in 1904 that the Orientals' idea of comfort far exceed ours." [17] She then recommended an imported "luxurious cane reading chair" made in the Orient for the piazza. [18]

Although most of the wicker furniture used in America was manufactured in the United States, the material itself was imported from China, Malaysia, and Japan—thus giving the wicker chair an inherent Oriental flavor. Wicker manufacturers enhanced this effect in the designs as well, for example, by incorporating such design elements as the Japanese fan into the chair backs.

The 1897 summer furniture catalogue of the Paine Furniture Company of Boston, one of the largest wicker manufacturers, capitalized on the appeal of the Oriental "idea of comfort." The introduction pointed out the growing popularity of wicker and discussed why if you wanted to achieve summer comfort it was the furniture to purchase. The wicker manufacturer's catalogue declared:

With each recurring year there is greater attention paid to summer pleasures. The hours of business have been shortened in all walks of life, and summer relaxation, which was once the luxury of the few, has become the law of the many. There is now a very large sale for summer furniture . . . First, it is cool and practical. Secondly, it is luxurious. Thirdly, it makes the home beautiful. Fourthly, it lasts for a quarter of a century. And finally, it costs almost nothing . . . [19]

The captions of the Paine Furniture Company's summer offerings noted wicker's oriental origins and stressed luxurious comfort. For example, one advertisement asserted that five minutes in an "East India Chair . . . [known commonly as a steamer chair] will rest you more than a half hour of ordinary chairing. It is the perfection of repose." [20]

A caption beneath wicker furnishings in the ordinary wide-weave style claimed that this furniture originated in the Azores and was discovered by invalids seeking recuperation. [21] A chaise in this style under the heading "Dreaming Wide Awake" promised: "The most sumptuous single article of summer furniture ever devised." [22]

Wicker was used as a railway car furnishing for summer excursion routes partly because of its resilience and partly because of the relaxed leisure atmosphere it helped to create. The traveller was escaping from the hectic city, seeking rest and relaxation in the country or by the seashore. Railroad advertising for summer excursions emphasized the comfort of the trains' facilities—citing among other features the presence of wicker furniture—and pictured representative examples of the individual cars.

The Pennsylvania Railroad Summer Excursion Routes pamphlet pictured two cars furnished in wicker, the Smoking and Library Car and Observation Car; which it said "duplicated for ladies and children the smoking compartment of the men." [23] (*Figure 6*) Bullinger's *Monitor Guide to Outing Trips and Tours* showed wicker in the Smoking and Library Car of the New York and Florida Short Line Limited. [24] An advertisement in *Century Magazine* for the Great Rock

63

(6)   The presence of wicker armchairs with rolled backs
and arms, one of the most popular varieties of
wicker available, on excursion trains underscored
for the traveller the kind of comfort he might
expect.   *The Pennsylvania Railroad Company,
Summer Excursion Routes (Philadelphia, 1891),*
p. 269

(7)   Summer houses contained wicker furniture for use
        both inside and outside, such as in the summer
        home of Mrs. Payne Whitney in Roslyn, Long
        Island.   *"The Works of Guy Lowell,"* The
        *Architectural Review (February 1906), v. XIII,
        no. 2, p. 38*

(8)   The lounging room at the Buckwood Inn in
        Shawnee-on-Delaware, Pennsylvania was furnished
        with one of the most popular varieties of wicker
        chair, the armchair with rolled arms and back.
        *The Architectural Review (April 1913), v. II, no.
        4, p. 151*

Island Route, which was described as "the favorite
Tourist Line to and from the Watering Places of the
Northwest, and the Sanitary and Scenic Resorts of Col-
orado" illustrated a dining car full of wicker chairs.[25]

Again wicker's resilient, lightweight and sturdy qualities made it popular for use on boats, particularly
yachts. The McHugh Willow Company even advertised
that it made wicker furniture designed especially for
yachts.[26] An article in *Harper's New Monthly Magazine*
entitled "The Social Side of Yachting" pictured several
wicker chairs on board. It was declared that yachting
was an ideal vacation; for "The leisure of the Man really
fond of the water and embarked for pleasure ought to
be unvexed, abundant; a holiday free from discordant
interruptions . . ." [27]

Once vacationers reached their destinations, whether
it was "a watering place of the Northwest" or a "scenic
resort of Colorado" they were likely to find their hotel
furnished with wicker. (*Figures 7-10*) Where and
how wicker was used at the resort hotel summarizes the
reasons for wicker's great popularity. Again as on the
train those areas in the hotel where it was important
that the furnishings provide both a comfortable relaxed
atmosphere and conveyed the impression that here you
were on vacation were the most likely to contain wicker
furniture. Hotel lobbies and reading rooms, for ex-

(9)   The Rotunda of the New Monmouth Hotel in
       Spring Lake, New Jersey contained the popular
       combination of furnishings—wicker chairs, palm
       trees, and Oriental style carpet.   The Architectural
       Review (April 1913), v. II, no. 4, p. 155

ample, were likely to contain large wicker chairs, with
rolled arms and backs—a style often referred to by the
wicker manufacturers as· the comfort rocker.

Wicker lent a touch of the romantic and exotic to
the ladies parlor, such as the Ladies Reading and Writing Room at the Hotel del Coronado or the Ladies
Assembly Room which was filled with comfort rockers
at the Arlington in Hot Springs, Arkansas. Sun parlors
or garden rooms in hotels such as the Windsor and
Haddon Hall of Atlantic City, New Jersey, were furnished with a variety of rattan furniture, which was
appropriate for the desired light and airy atmosphere
of these rooms.[28] City hotels also capitalized on the
exotic atmosphere provided by wicker furniture and
often had at least one room furnished with this practical
furniture. The rattan chairs were usually accompanied
by an abundance of palm trees, again a reference to the
outdoors as well as an added hint of the Oriental origins
of the wicker.

(10)   The Palm Room at the Garden City Hotel in
       Garden City, Long Island was an addition in 1913
       to the original McKin, Mead & White hotel and it
       was decorated with the popular resort style
       furnishings—wicker.   The Architectural Review
       (April 1913), v. II, no. 4, p. 144

Wicker invoked an atmosphere of rest and repose throughout the second half of the nineteenth century and the first quarter of the twentieth century. In fact, wicker was so successful as a vacation furniture that the same arbiters of taste who recommended it for summer houses and verandas soon were recommending it for year-round use to provide a bright "summery look." [29]

The Decorator and Furnisher wrote in 1893: "Why should rattan or reed furniture be used exclusively in summer cottages: its usefulness is quite as proper, quite as fashionable in the city dwelling as in a cottage located on the seashore, or in the mountains . . . There is no reason, in fact, why cane furniture should not become permanently used in every household, seeing that it combines lightness, elegance, usefulness and cheapness." [30]

NOTES

[1] Andrew Jackson Downing, The Architecture of Country Houses (New York and Philadelphia, 1850), p. 409.

[2] Ibid., p. 410.

[3] Gervase Wheeler, Rural Homes (New York, 1851), p. 190.

[4] Ibid., p. 190.

[5] Ibid., p. 197.

[6] Tyrrell Ward & Company, How to Furnish Your Home and Clothe Yourself Without Cost (Chicago: Rogers and Hall Company Press, 1900), p. 44.

[7] Advertisement, "Mellin's Baby Food," Ladies Home Journal (June 1898), p. 23.

[8] Ralph Henry Barbour, Heart's Content (Philadelphia, 1915), p. 92.

[9] Carrie May Ashton, "Fads and Fashions," The American Home Journal (March 1898), II, no. 5, p. 160.

[10] Advertisement, Wakefield Rattan Company, Scribner's Monthly (June 1881), p. 10.

[11] Paine's Furniture Company, Rattan and Reed Furniture (Boston, 1891), no. 8820A.

[12] "Decorative Notes," The Decorator and Furnisher (August 1892), p. 186.

[13] "Summer Furnishing," The Decorator and Furnisher (July 1893), p. 148.

[14] Ibid., p. 144.

[15] Ibid., p. 149.

[16] Harriet Prescott Spofford, Art Decoration Applied to Furniture (New York, 1878), p. 166.

[17] The House and Home: A Practical Book, Vol. 2 (New York, 1896), p. 160.

[18] Ibid., p. 160.

[19] Paine Furniture Company, Summer Furniture (Boston, 1897), p. 2.

[20] Ibid., p. 14.

[21] Ibid., p. 16.

[22] Ibid., p. 18.

[23] Pennsylvania Railroad Company, Summer Excursion Routes (Philadelphia, 1891), p. 269.

[24] E. W. Bullinger, Outing Trips and Tours (New York, 1895), p. 29.

[25] Advertisement, The Great Rock Island Route, Century Magazine (August 1890), p. 77.

[26] Advertisement, Joseph P. McHugh and Son, The Architectural Record (March 1915), p. 45.

[27] J. D. Jerrold Kelley, "The Social Side of Yachting," Harper's New Monthly Magazine (August 1890), p. 593.

[28] Hotel Del Coronado (San Diego County, 1890), p. 11. The Hot Springs of Arkansas and its Great Hotels: The Arlington and Eastman (Hot Springs, 1900), p. 24. The Hotel Windsor (Atlantic City, New Jersey), garden room. Hadden Hall, Atlantic City, New Jersey (Philadelphia), sun parlor. Pamphlets, The Henry Francis du Pont Winterthur Museum Library.

[29] The Decorator and Furnisher (April 1885), p. 26.

[30] "Summer Furnishings," The Decorator and Furnisher (June 1893), p. 108.

CRACKER RESORTS

Lee H. Warner

CRACKER RESORTS

Lee H. Warner

FLORIDA IS A TWENTIETH-CENTURY PHENOMENON. Even though the state joined the Union in 1845, it remained underpopulated and largely ignored by most Americans until after World War I. And until the state had its image and character firmly fixed, there were years of groping and searching for an identity in a location that was unlike other settled portions of the Union.

By the mid-nineteenth century a typically American southern frontier community existed on the northern rim of Florida, gathered around three growing towns—St. Augustine, Pensacola, and Tallahassee. Tallahassee, youngest of the three, lay twenty miles inland and for most of the century was without easy communication with the rest of the nation or, for that matter, other parts of Florida. Partly as a result, the inhabitants took on a set of characteristics which, although not unlike other populations in similar circumstances, set them apart. They were called crackers, although that term would not apply equally to all people in the area. (Certainly those in the top rank of the society would resist that identification.)

Crackers were those north Floridians—either native-born or outlanders of long residence—who shared a heightened skepticism of visitors and other sections of the country. They were defiantly independent, agrarian and, in a relative sense, without wealth. These characteristics were strengthened by the South's defeat in the Civil War, but their beginnings are obvious much earlier.

The first wave of Tallahasseeans had distinct origins. Most of those who would occupy society's upper ranks were from the upper South, especially Virginia. William Du Val, territorial governor, was from the old Dominion as was Thomas Brown, second elected governor, and Francis Eppes, Thomas Jefferson's grandson. From Maryland and Virginia came William Wirt's

sons-in-law, the Randalls and Gambles. The Calls and Walkers came from Kentucky. North Carolina produced Chaires, Crooms and Branchs. They were conservative, patrician, and usually, Episcopalian.[1]

They were the kind of people who had confronted leisure time in their past. They continued their well-worn habits, as might be expected, and tended to spend their summers either at traditional upper-south watering places or well-known northern resorts. As one romantic reminiscence of the moonlight and magnolia school put it,

The social life of the South was not entirely within the home; every summer preparations began early in the season for a general flitting to "The Springs" or perhaps instead of the springs, it was the sea-side. In either case the getting ready was a work of time. Orders were sent to New York, dressmakers were called in, the home seamstresses were put to work and much studying of styles from Godey's Ladies Book. Trying on, careful fitting, the tucks, the frills, the shirrings, flowers-appliqued on silken robes, the finest of lace-trimmed lingerie, and real lace at that, for an imitation in lace or jewels was not permissable.[2]

There were enough confirming accounts to make the story believable in outline at least, if not in detail. There were "reports that the county of Leon [Tallahassee] is well represented, both at Shocks's Springs and the Virginia Green Briar." And, as one well-connected Tallahasseean wrote home from White Sulphur, "Judge Allen, G[eorge] K. Walker and G[eorge] T. Ward are here, dancing attendance on the fair, coming and going with fine establishments.... There are numbers of people here—the very best of Virginia's best."[3] Besides these best known of Southern places, trips to Niagara Falls, Saratoga and New York City were not unknown among middle Floridians, as were extended stays at Old Point Comfort and other Southern spots.[4]

But, at the same time, there began to be attractions closer to home. The reasons are not hard to divine. Time, expense and ease of travel were obvious difficulties with the traditional resorts. As well, there was the beginning of an appreciation of the attractive qualities of the home region.

"I would rather take my ease at home," explained one resident who was becoming a cracker, "as he thrust a knife into the green side of a forty pound, red hearted watermelon." The reasons? "What mountain air or spring water could compensate for the want of figs and cream during the summer? Anyhow, there are sulphur springs all over Florida; one not twenty miles from here." But then came the substantial reason, the one that would go far toward creating the twentieth century retirement villages, Gold Coast, Disney World, Anita Bryant and Florida orange juice: "The fact is, there is a sort of watering place tone of things existing here all the year round—a pleasing *abandon*." [5]

The specific impetus to a home grown resort, however, was more urgent—if less direct. In 1841 yellow fever struck and literally decimated Tallahassee. In an effort to escape the horrible reality of the disease whose cause they did not comprehend, the socially prominent and wealthy built a summer community four miles south of Tallahassee on the piney-woods flatlands. The town was known as Bel Air, where, one resident remembered, "health secured, it . . . [became] a summer resort with our social world." Limited almost exclusively to well-to-do Whigs (Democrats contemptuously referred to it as "Scratch Ankle.") it became a summer refuge that lasted until the War. It was so popular among upper class Tallahasseeans that the Episcopal church built a chapel there for use during the season.

Despite the popular image of the southern piney-woods flatlands, in a pre-air conditioning, pre-refrigeration world it must have been very pleasant. "Hither the hero's and nymphs resort," one account ran, "to taste the pleasures of social chat in evening rambles, bee's teas and tableaux,—cards, lunch, music, concentrated by the hospitable forces of the country." [6]

It was a community of cottages, almost all privately owned. The only community buildings seem to have been the Episcopal chapel and, later for some who became permanent residents, a school. There were no outsiders: it was the social elite of Tallahassee in their summer pattern. Likewise, the existence of Bel Air did not preclude their summer travel to established resorts further north. It simply provided an alternative and helped to build the notion that Florida, too, had something to offer in the way of summer respite.

But the world of Old Point Comfort, the Green Briar and Bel Air was not to last—at least for Tallahasseeans. The Civil War interfered. Twentieth century Floridians point with pride to the fact that Tallahassee was the only Confederate capitol east of the Mississippi

which was not captured by Union troops. But that oversight ought not obscure the suffering and misery of Tallahasseeans during and, especially, after the war. The economic devastation was real: all financial paper, including currency, was suddenly without value. The federal government confiscated all baled cotton and imposed a heavy tax to drain off much of what wealth remained. Thus, at precisely the time when capital was necessary to reinvigorate the faltering economy, money was instead withdrawn from the South. As well, political and social conditions were so chaotic that monied Yankee entrepreneurs were leary of making investments.

This situation insured that for a twenty-year period there was no talk and probably no thought of summer resorts in Tallahassee and other places like it. The class which heretofore had been able to afford such luxury was now suffering economic repression; the transportation network had been destroyed and it was much too soon for Northerners to be interested in Southern winters.

Although the solid—and opulent—revival of the Southern economy and the resulting rebirth of social life would not come until the 1880s, there were precursors. Some bordered on the pathetic: "the property on Cat Point advertised as the 'Guano works,' has been purchased by parties in Tallahassee, with the design of erecting a summer hotel thereon." [7] Other moves, however, showed careful analysis and planning. The most noteworthy of these was an attempt to secure a first-class hotel for Tallahassee. [8]

In many ways the desire for a new Tallahassee hotel was an attempt to cut in (and cash in) on the boom that was beginning in Thomasville, Georgia, Tallahassee's neighbor across the state line. Because it was convenient to important north-south railroad lines and other transportation routes, and as a result of some very favorable publicity, Thomasville had become identified as a popular winter resort. The identification continued for a generation, reaching its peak when President William McKinley spent his winter vacations there. [9]

In Tallahassee, the movement culminated with the building of the Leon Hotel in 1883, just in time to catch the revival of the Southern economy. (*Figure 1*) A three story wooden structure, it initially had sixty "sleeping rooms and private parlors" advertised as hav-

(1) **The Leon Hotel, 1906.** *Florida Photographic Archives, Strozier Library, Florida State University*

(2) **Main staircase of the Leon Hotel, 1906.** *Florida Photographic Archives, Strozier Library, Florida State University*

ing "every modern convenience" including "water and gas throughout the entire structure." For long-depressed cracker Tallahassee, it was imposing from its grand stairway to its private ladies parlors.[10] (Figure 2)

For some years the Leon evidently did draw northern visitors. It closed for the summer, as any respectable resort hotel in the South, and seems to have had an acceptable occupancy rate during the season for travel. But ultimately it was not to become a resort palace. Those northerners who were looking for a short-term resort were more likely to go to the better-known Thomasville—especially after President McKinley went there. Northerners who were interested in hunting usually wanted to own their own property and became semi-permanent residents—a resort hotel was not for them. Finally, of course, there was nothing particularly significant about Tallahassee. For all its pre-War social pretensions, the Civil War and Reconstruction shattered any dreams of prestige and opulence.

In the end, it would be the establishments that grew up along the Gulf coast—a few miles south of Tallahassee—that would become Florida's cracker resorts. Patronage would be largely confined to families within one day's travel of the area and would be limited to the summer months—unlike the hotels that began to spring up along Flagler's railroad on Florida's east coast. In any case, Tallahasseeans of position and means now began to go to the Gulf Coast rather than northward for the summer.[11] They went to establishments that emphasized beaches or mineral springs that abounded in the area, and which were modeled on their better-known and infinitely more luxurious and comfortable northern counterparts.

Getting there, to places like Panacea, St. Theresa or Lanark, was a challenge in itself. In the case of Panacea, you "took the train to Sopchoppy and then you were met there by the tramcar." The tramcar was "a covered wagon with steps at the back and seats down either side;" it was pulled by two mules and ran on a track made out of crossties laid end to end. To make the trip even more difficult, "the sand was so deep, [that] the mules couldn't pull that heavy load," and, unfortunately, the passengers had to get out and walk the hills. As one rider remembered, "it took ages ... to get from Sopchoppy to Panacea."[12] Denials to the contrary, it was a rigorous trip[13] (Figure 3)

The trip was all the more arduous because it required substantial amounts of baggage and supplies. Most families traveled to the coast to spend three months at a time: because the area was so isolated, all the more was required. "Seafood of most any kind was there for the taking," but there were no groceries available. Some families took flour by the barrel; others took

chickens and occasionally a cow. Everyone took a variety of canned goods."[14]

Each of the three resort communities had a hotel; at St. Theresa there were private cottages; Panacea and St. Theresa had boarding houses. Lanark and Panacea both advertised mineral springs and all three provided easy access to the beach and swimming. Lanark, built by the Scottish Land Improvement Company and located on a railroad main line, was easily the most complete and best known of the three.

The hotels, like almost all buildings in north Florida, were frame, two story structures. (Figure 4) Verandahs and galleries seemed to be everywhere. All guest rooms had windows and by the 1890s were served with gas lighting. The Lanark hotel boasted that each room was connected to the office "by an electric bell" and "provided with spring beds, hair mattresses and all modern conveniences."[15]

The Lanark spring was well advertised for its drinking qualities. "When freshly drawn, the sense of smell and taste at once detect the presence of sulphur. It is alkaline on reaction, evidently containing sulphates of lime and magnesia." Doctors recommended it "for indigestion and dyspepsia" and as well, for rheumatism.[16] At Panacea "there were five different springs and each was supposed to have certain medicinal qualities." Patrons would partake of whichever medicinal spring seemed most appropriate to the individual. But, at Panacea, there were also mineral bath pools for soaking."[17]

Because the hotels were on the Gulf of Mexico, swimming and beach activities were popular. The best swimming seems to have been at Lanark. There a boardwalk led from the hotel to the pier. On the pier were "two large bath houses for ladies and gentlemen respectively, each being fitted with private dressing rooms for the bathers."[18] The bath houses were totally enclosed.

Other activities were normal for that time and place. Lanark advertised that "a fine fleet of pleasure boats ... [was] provided for the hotel guests and the fishing ... cannot be surpassed on the coast." At Panacea, there was a billiard and shuffle board room and everywhere, of course, there were the organized picnics and excursions, either secular or organized by churches.[19]

By current standards of leisure activities, obviously, it was primitive; compared to the facilities and activities in more traditional northern resorts—or even the newly built Florida east coast or old New Orleans resorts—the comparison would have undoubtedly been the same. It was raw and isolated. (Figure 5)

But the families who went there each summer remembered it fondly. To some extent, the fond mem-

ories are simply the romantic ones of older people reminiscing and clouding harsher realities. But the memories had a substantial basis in reality. Many of the cottages still exist, the beaches are still attractive and, more important, the families went back year after year: their reasons confirm the thought.

"I remember one particular time," one lady recalled, when her mother and a Mrs. Fitzgerald chaperoned a group of girls at a house party. "Of course the young men . . . that were the particular friends or sweethearts, as the case might be, of the girls that were down there" would also come to the coast but stayed at the hotel. "One night one of the boys sent this girl in a five pound box of candy and when she opened it it was full of fiddler crabs." Surprise, the girl dropped it and "screamed and the fiddlers ran all over the house and I can see Mrs. Fitzgerald to this day with a broom." She would "wack up the fiddler and try to brush it out and then she'd scream and then she'd go after it again. It was much excitement for a long time before we got all those fiddlers out of the house." [20]

In a less exciting vein, "the Greek boats would come in and anchor at the dock and put the oysters in the water." For ten cents "the sailor would open you a dozen oysters and you sat on the little box on the boat and ate the oysters out of the shell by suction, which is really the way to eat oysters on the half shell you know." Then, more to the point, "I was crazy about oysters and the older girls would get to talking to the man and I would get my dozen oysters and part of theirs and they never knew the difference." [21]

Or, "we children would take pins with us and lay them on the tracks and make scissors, spell out your name with pins, and when the train ran over it, it would mash them together. We'd go to the store and get soda water and zoozoos and sit there on the counter and eat. That was a very exciting time." [22]

It was exciting, obviously, only if you were very young and lived in the sheltered, parochial north Florida cracker community. But in the stories and memories of the families and friends who frequented the cracker resorts of Victorian Florida lay the germ of today's Florida. It was, as the early publicist concluded, "a sort

(3) Tram Road to Panacea. *Florida Photographic Archives, Strozier Library, Florida State University*

(4) Panacea Hotel. *Florida Photographic Archives, Strozier Library, Florida State University*

(5) Patrick Houston, his party, and the staff of the Panacea Hotel pose for the photograph. *Florida Photographic Archives, Strozier Library, Florida State University.*

of watering place tone of things existing" there "all the year round." And when north-south transportation lines became better developed, and travel and leisure activities came within the reach of a majority of Americans in the twentieth century, the retirement villages, the Gold Coast, Disney World, Anita Bryant and Florida orange juice would displace the cracker resorts.

NOTES

[1] *Fifth Census, 1830*, Population Schedules, Florida, Leon County, pp. 1–8; *Sixth Census, 1840*, Population Schedules, Florida Leon County, pp. 76–80. Bertram Groene, *Antebellum Tallahassee* (Tallahassee: Florida Heritage Foundation, 1971), pp. 41–71, provides a convenient reference for settler's starting points. On the matter of being Episcopalian, see the "Parrish Register" of St. John's Episcopal Church, Tallahassee, Florida.

[2] Susan Bradford Eppes, *Through Some Eventful Years* (1926; reprint ed., Gainesville, Florida: University of Florida Press, 1968), pp. 16–17.

[3] Ellen Call Long, *Florida Breezes: or Florida New and Old* (1883; reprint ed., Gainesville, Florida: University of Florida Press, 1962), p. 178. See also the Oral History Transcript of Mrs. John Ward Henderson, Sr. in the Florida State Archives, pp. 6–7.

[4] Eppes, *Through Some Eventful Years*, pp. 18, 68–9, 76–7.

[5] Long, *Florida Breezes*, pp. 178-79.

[6] *Ibid.*, pp. 2466–47; Groene, *Antebellum Tallahassee*, pp. 54–55.

[7] Weekly *Floridian*, 20 January and 7 July 1874.

[8] *Ibid.*, 19 December 1875, 21 November 1876, 21 August 1877, 27 August, 3 December 1878.

[9] The best summary of the winter resort era in Thomasville is in William W. Rogers, *Thomas County, 1865–1900* (Tallahassee: Florida State University Press, 1973), pp. 131–52, 331–44.

[10] Weekly *Floridian*, 14 March 1882.

[11] Oral History Transcript of George E. Lewis, Florida State Archives (unpaged).

[12] Oral History Transcript of Annie Sensabaugh, Florida State Archives, p. 10; Oral History Transcript, Henderson, p. 6.

[13] Message on postcard in Florida State Photographic Archives, Florida State University, filed under title "Tram Road to Panacea."

[14] Oral History Transcript of Alma Elizabeth Moor Bradford, Florida State Archives, p. 14; Oral History Transcript, Sensabaugh, pp. 15–16; Oral History Transcript, Henderson, p. 7.

[15] Pamphlet with title page missing, cataloged under title *Leon and Wakulla Counties* in Florida State Library, Tallahassee, p. 11.

[16] *Leon and Wakulla Counties*, p. 12.

[17] Photograph in *Leon and Wakulla Counties*.

[18] *Leon and Wakulla Counties*, p. 11.

[19] Oral History Transcript, Sensabaugh, p. 14.

[20] *Ibid.*, pp. 12–13.

[21] *Ibid.*, p. 14.

[22] *Ibid.*, pp. 16–17.

THE TRUE CARLSBAD OF AMERICA:
THE HOTEL BROADWATER AND NATATORIUM OF
HELENA, MONTANA

Patricia Dean

(2) Charles A. Broadwater, 1890. *Montana Historical Society*

THE TRUE CARLSBAD OF AMERICA:
THE HOTEL BROADWATER AND NATATORIUM OF
HELENA, MONTANA

Patricia Dean

HORTLY AFTER the Hotel Broadwater and Natatorium of Helena, Montana opened in 1889, an overwhelmed visitor wrote:

The self-contained New Yorker would think it only a western yarn if you should tell him how really elegant the Broadwater is, with the largest and finest bath house in the world, gay with music, tropical with huge palms near which a mimic waterfall dashes down many feet and supplied with creative water from hot springs of 160° heat. Though now the fame of it is going abroad all over the land, the provincial New Yorker will probably be the last to hear of it. The hotel is piped all over with this hot mineral water . . . the grounds about the hotel are beautifully laid out and oh! such views of the mountains, such fishing not far away, such electric air! [1]

Some might have judged the costly erection of this extravagant resort in the wilds of Montana as the most foolhardy venture imaginable. (*Figure 1*) To an individual such as Colonel Charles A. Broadwater, whose fortunes had grown with those of the territory, the construction of the Hotel Broadwater and Natatorium was the natural culmination of his career.

Broadwater was born in 1840 and grew up on his parents' cotton plantation near St. Louis. (*Figure 2*) When he was twenty-one years old Colorado beckoned and he spent two years there before moving to Virginia City, Montana where he handled a pack train for a freight company. Charles Broadwater worked as a superintendent for the outfit and eventually became a partner. The days of the freighter were coming to an end with the advent of the railroad, however, and he moved his family to Helena where he assumed the presidency of the Montana National Bank and also engaged in contracting. In 1886 he became president of the Montana Central Line, a division of J. J. Hill's Great Northern Railway. Contemporary biographers cite Broadwater's faith in Helena's future as the reason for the resort's construction and this is certainly a plausible explanation.

By 1890 Helena, known as "the Queen City of the Rockies," boasted 13,834 citizens, five public schools, three parochial schools, two business colleges, one university under construction and twelve churches. Deposits in the city's four national banks exceeded those found in the banks of Portland, Seattle, Spokane, Salt Lake City, or Tacoma.[2] Only twenty-six years had passed between the discovery of gold in Last Chance Gulch which established Helena and the city's distinction of having the wealthiest per capita population in the world.[3]

To the younger generation Helena is a Parisian-like center . . . Its surroundings, even its society, largely comprised of Eastern and college-bred men and young wives fresh from older centers, are delightfully prominent features . . . Helena, in the truest sense of the word, is cosmopolitan.[4]

And, like any other nineteenth century cosmopolitan center, Helena required a resort, a spot where one could bathe away the infirmities and strain of a toilsome workday, a place where one could recover the energy necessary to deal with the demands tomorrow's busy world would undoubtedly bring.

In the late summer of 1888 ground was broken for the new resort at Ten-Mile Hot Springs, two miles outside of Helena. Charles Broadwater selected John C. Paulsen and Noah J. McConnell, noted local architects, to design the Natatorium. Paulsen, the senior partner, was German-born and had studied at the schools of architecture in Hanover, Stuttgart, and Berlin. After serving in military construction work during the Franco-Prussian War, he designed exhibitions in Vienna, Zurich, and Paris. Paulsen decided to stay in the United States while visiting and in 1887 moved to Montana where he eventually became State Architect. Less is known about Paulsen's partner, Noah J. McConnell, who was born in New York City in 1855. When he was eighteen McConnell left for San Francisco where he worked in construction for two years before moving to Black Hills, South Dakota. Once there he gave up construction work and became a newspaper correspondent but apparently this held no great interest for two years later he relocated to Butte, Montana. Finally, after nine years of mining in Butte he moved to Helena and joined John C. Paulsen and Company as an architect and superintendent.

The resort also needed a hotel and Broadwater chose Herman Kemna to design it. Kemna, who had only lived in Helena for one year, was possibly known to Broadwater through his drafting work for the Northern Pacific Railroad, Montana Central's competitor.

Originally the resort was to open in early June 1889 but construction ran behind schedule from the beginning. Work on the Natatorium's superstructure only commenced that spring. A local newspaperman visited the Natatorium's construction site and reported:

the design is Moorish and when finished the building will be an architectural gem. It will be something like a greenhouse exteriorly made up of walls that are largely comprised of glass. There will be 12,000 square feet of glass used in its construction, half of which will be stained glass and half plain. Under the magnificent canopy will be the great plunge bath, a basin 300 x 80 feet in dimensions and about 8' deep and lined with cement.[5]

Construction continued through May and June at a hectic pace with 275 men at work building the hotel. When that building was completed the labor force was to hurriedly finish the Natatorium for the grand opening on July third. By June thirteenth however, Broadwater realized his resort would not be open until midsummer but work did not slacken. Finally on 26 August 1889 the Hotel Broadwater opened to the public.

The hotel, built of wood from Oregon and Minnesota, was a two-story cottage-like building. (*Figure 3*) A tower, porches and balconies afforded guests a variety of locations for viewing the scenic wonders of the Prickly Pear Valley and Continental Divide. Verandas measuring eighteen feet wide and extending nearly one-quarter mile across the building's front were lit with electric lamps, as was the entire hotel. These vantage points not only offered spectacular scenery but other pleasures too, as Henry James described in "An International Episode":

In front was a gigantic veranda upon which an army might have camped—a vast wooden terrace with a roof as lofty as the nave of a cathedral. Here . . . American society . . . was distributed over the measureless expanse . . . and appeared to consist largely of pretty girls, dressed as if for a fête champêtre, swaying to and fro in rocking chairs.[6]

The hotel's interior belied its modest clapboard exterior. Unfortunately few interior photographs exist but descriptions abound extolling the good quality and

(1) Hotel Broadwater and Natatorium, c. 1890. *Montana Historical Society*

craftsmanship of the furnishings and fittings. Capable of sleeping hundreds, the hostelry had ten suites with private baths and fireplaces, approximately fifty guest rooms with a marble sink in every one, a spacious lobby, three ornamental staircases, a ballroom, billiard hall, barber shop, two parlors with ornate solid cherry woodwork, and 160 stained glass windows. Etchings and engravings, Turkish rugs and tapestries, furniture of mahogany, oak, cherry and walnut filled the hotel's rooms. The hotel's forty bathrooms possessed the establishment's most luxurious appointments: silver-trimmed porcelain tubs on marble feet costing $200 apiece and imported from Paris. The Broadwater also offered two small plunges within the hotel building itself for those guests who were anxious to experience the benefits of the celebrated mineral water but who were disinclined to visit the Natatorium. Vapor baths, douche sprays, and needle shower completed the hotel's bathing facilities. Water piped from the hot springs met all the resort's bathing and heating needs.

A ten-foot coal range, commodious walk-in meat cooler and bakery with brick oven outfitted the kitchen while the laundry, housed in a brick structure adjacent to the hotel, was said to be "supplied with every facility, and in short everything needed for a hotel."[7]

Nearly five hundred people, including the city council and mayor, attended the evening opening, traveling to the hot springs by carriage or the city motor line. A thirty-eight course dinner was served in the dining room from six to ten p.m. Reed and Barton silver and cutlery engraved with the establishment's name shone on the damask tablecloths. One hundred fifty guests seated in the three dining rooms were simultaneously served by "the dining room force . . . composed of colored waiters, who went expertly about their task attired in full-dress suits."[8]

The Capital City Band played during dinner and those who had finished the nocturnal repast danced on the verandas, savoring the evening's coolness. Rustic benches, winding paths illuminated by incandescent lights, and flowerbeds and fountains dotted the resort's forty acres.

The Natatorium had been scheduled to open with the hotel but its debut was postponed due to a leak. At last on August 28, the Natatorium, judged by some to

(3) **Hotel Broadwater, c. 1890. *Montana Historical Society***

be "the finest specimen of Moorish architecture in the world"[9] opened its doors to the public. (*Figures 4 and 5*) The Plunge, as it was popularly known, took full advantage of the natural hot springs found in the area. Three pipes supplied water to the bathing pool which measured three hundred feet long and eighty feet wide. One million gallons of water a day rushed over a forty-foot high mass of granite boulders. A stairway cut into the rock wound to the top of the tower where twenty people could stand together and survey the pool. Electric lights placed between the rocks transformed the showering water into a glittering, prismatic cascade. Swings, toboggan slides, ladders and springboards surrounded the pool where novice and expert swimmer alike frolicked before retiring to the steam-heated dressing rooms. However relaxed the atmosphere at the Natatorium might have seemed to be, care was taken to observe propriety and ensure respectability.

For fifty cents man, woman, or child can rent a bathing suit, have a comfortable dressing room and bathe in the buoyant hot spring water . . . Rules are strict and rigidly enforced against boisterous conduct, loud talking, or swearing in the bath, and no intoxicated person is permitted to enter it. Any lady or gentleman can visit the bath at any time without fear of insult or offense.[10]

In the first week of September the Plunge closed for the season and Broadwater set about putting the finishing touches on his three hundred thousand dollar enterprise. Owing to its hasty completion, the hostelry's grounds resembled more a forsaken desert than the tree-shaded lovers' paradise that befitted such an elegant retreat. Rambles and walkways wound throughout the grounds where fountains like "The Boy with the Leaky Boot" played. C. L. Lewis, secretary of the Minnesota State Forestry Association and Life Member of the Minnesota State Horticultural Society, took charge of the landscaping. Twenty-five varieties of native trees and shrubs guaranteed to be "perfectly hardy as far north as Manitoba" arrived at the Broadwater in several railroad cars from Minnesota nurseries and experimental farms.[11] Twenty-two varieties of sturdy Russian trees were also shipped. Maples, boxelders, birches, poplars, cherry and walnut trees, white willows, tamaracks, honeysuckle, ivy and twelve-year old elm trees fifteen inches in diameter and thirty-five feet high soon transformed the grounds. Four thousand tulip, crocus, and hyacinth bulbs decorated the wide expanses of green lawn. The Natatorium received tropical trees and plants in addition to one thousand tuberoses.

---

(4) Natatorium, c. 1890. *Montana Historical Society*

(5) Natatorium interior, date unknown. *Montana Historical Society*

A few hundred yards northwest of the Natatorium a hole one-third mile long and twelve feet deep was dug. The creation of Lake Thermal allowed hotel visitors to engage in boating, ice-skating and other seasonal aquatic sports. A friend of Broadwater's sent him a stuffed swan to ornament the lake.

The hostelry's first year ended on a festive note at an extravagant Christmas dinner serving lobster, suckling pig, sea bass, roast pheasant, English plum pudding, and other delectables.

Although Charles Broadwater became best known for his resort, he was still a bank and railroad president. In 1892, he traveled East on business. While in New York City he came down with influenza and returned to Helena in time to see the opening of the resort's third season. On 24 May 1892, Charles Broadwater died in his private suite at the hotel. His funeral several days later was the largest ever held in Montana at that time. Special trains ran from nearby cities and five thousand people attended.

The hotel lobbies, the verandas, and the walks were all but black with humanity . . . In the West Side Parlor of the hotel the body of Colonel Broadwater was resting in a black-covered casket surrounded by masses of flowers in various designs . . . After rendering 'Nearer My God to Thee', the hotel band played a funeral march composed for the occasion by the leader . . . the balconies and lawns thronged with people, a semi-circle of carriages running far into the highway and broken by a line of white-aproned Masons and yet not a sound save the music of the band.[12]

Broadwater's death was but the beginning of the resort's woes. Immediately after his demise rumors speculating upon the hostelry's closure prompted the newspaper to publish the manager's assurance that this season at the Broadwater was to be a profitable one. The 1892 season ended early however and the following year the resort opened late. The Panic of 1893 did little to help and finally, in 1894, the hotel closed. The only profit-making part of the resort, the Plunge continued to operate.

In the meantime, the world for which Colonel Broadwater had built his establishment was rapidly changing. By 1900 Helena had relinquished its title as Montana's largest city to Butte, copper supplier to the nation. Ironically, it was a Brooklyn-born mining engineer from Butte who tried to save the Broadwater Hotel. F. Augustus Heinze, a graduate of the Columbia School of Mines, had come to Butte in 1889 and left for Wall Street fifteen years later—a millionaire at the age of thirty-five. Sometime in the winter of 1906–1907 Heinze bought the Broadwater and opened the hotel for a winter season. Advertisements urged potential visitors to see "Real Life through Broadwater Eyes" and that

The True Carlsbad of America . . . offered a haven to the invalid, a luxurious resort to those who tire of commonplace humdrum. Social events of the state will circulate around this famous hostelry the present winter.[13]

The hotel's idle years had led to deterioration and much work had to be done before it could reopen. Walls and ceilings were replastered, the dining room was remodeled, and new carpets and furniture were installed. On 4 January 1907 the Broadwater Hotel was officially reopened and many of Colonel Broadwater's old friends were present. Many who attended the event reflected that Broadwater's death presaged the decline of the Capital City and perhaps Heinze's acquisition of the resort meant better days could not be far ahead.

A month later Heinze unveiled his plans for improvements at the Broadwater. A brick addition containing two hundred guest rooms, ballroom, and gymnasium would insure its popularity and profitability as a year-round resort. In the winter months, the Natatorium was to convert into a roller-skating rink reverting in spring, summer and autumn to the popular swimming spot it had become. The success of the rejuvenated resort depended upon the railroads which served Montana's other large cities, Butte and Great Falls. Heinze, however, remained convinced that the Broadwater would prosper due solely to its merits and promised: "Butte will send thousands every month during summer to the Broadwater and every city in the state will contribute to the success of the first year of its re-opening." [14]

In the meantime, Heinze's Wall Street success came to an end when he was indicted for misapplication of bank funds and was sued for one million dollars in promissory note payments. He was acquitted and later regained some of his wealth but apparently the Broadwater resort and proposed connecting railroad lines were lost as a result. Seven years later, the forty-five-year-old Heinze died of cirrhosis of the liver while vacationing at another famous resort, Saratoga Springs.

A number of owners succeeded Heinze until 1919 when Helena raised one hundred thousand dollars by public subscription to purchase and operate the hotel. Forty-five tent cottages were erected on the grounds to attract tourists traveling by auto from Yellowstone Park to Glacier National Park. DeWitt Hutchings, an owner/manager of Riverside, California's Mission Inn, came to Helena to manage the hotel and its eighty-five employees. The resort's season from June 10 to September 20 lasted 90 days. Once again, the hotel was repaired and refurbished while advertisements emphasized the healthful qualities of the mineral water found at the Plunge.

(6) Hotel Broadwater, c. 1939. *Montana Historical Society*

Apparently the anticipated guests failed to appear for in 1920 Charles B. Power, a descendant of one of Montana's early merchant princes, bought the Broadwater and operated the hotel as a restaurant for the next seventeen years. An earthquake in the late 1930s severely damaged the Natatorium and forced its closure. In 1938 Power sold the resort. (*Figure 6*) Renamed the Broadwater Inn, most of the hotel was sealed off although dining and dancing to such bands as "'Mal' Duke and His Royal Hawaiians" continued. After a statewide crackdown on gambling in 1941, the Broadwater closed.

During World War II it appeared as if the Broadwater might be reopened as a rest and relaxation location for soldiers; but the one hundred thousand dollars apportioned by the War Department for the resort's restoration went to build a memorial park instead. In 1945 a local man bought the resort for $25,000. He reroofed the hotel building and intended to use the Natatorium as an outdoor pool. But, as before, the necessary financial backing fell through and in 1946 the Natatorium was razed.

For the next twenty-eight years the hotel and the Natatorium ruins evoked little more than passerbys' curiosity and futile laments until the owner was forced to auction the hotel's contents and raze whatever parts of the building remained unsold.

So many other fine buildings whose presence symbolized dreams fulfilled and dreams forgotten have disappeared in the dusty blur of the wrecker's ball or the din of explosives strategically, destructively placed within their walls. The Broadwater did not deserve such a fate, its past magnificence unappreciated, its end unobserved.

The Helena Symphony Society was given permission to conduct guided tours through the building. Thousands paid two dollars apiece to wander the overgrown grounds and marvel at the elegance and spaciousness that characterize times a few could remember only faintly, and many could do little but read and dream about. The auction was well-attended, each successful bidder taking a treasured piece of stained glass, woodwork, or even a porch or tower home with him.

Today the Broadwater is gone. Pieces and parts of it do remain in Helena though; one of the hotel's porches sits in a yard, carefully restored and lovingly appreciated. The observation tower rests in one corner of a local schoolyard, no doubt evoking much the same comment it did when it graced the long, low roofline of the Hotel Broadwater.

Perhaps the most perceptive observation made about the Hotel Broadwater and Natatorium is to be found in the 1889 *Helena City Directory*:

It seems the development of these springs till the present day has been deferred no doubt for some wise purpose, probably more forcibly to emphasize in full measure Berkeley's prophecy:

> Westward the course of empire takes its way;
> The first four acts already past,
> A fifth shall close the drama with the day
> Time's noblest *hot springs* is the last.[15]

NOTES

[1] *The Northwest Magazine* (June 1890), p. 21.

[2] *Helena City Directory* (St. Paul: R. L. Polk and Company, 1890), p. 53½.

[3] *Helena Weekly Herald* (29 August 1889), p. 5.

[4] Edward Roberts, "Two Montana Cities," *Harper's New Monthly Magazine* (September 1888), pp. 585–87.

[5] *Helena Weekly Herald* (25 April 1889), p. 8.

[6] "Design Notebook," *New York Times* (28 June 1979) Sec. C, p. 10.

[7] *Helena Daily Independent* (27 August 1889), p. 8.

[8] *Helena Weekly Herald* (29 August 1889), p. 7.

[9] *Great Northern Bulletin* (Summer 1892), p. 2.

[10] *Helena Daily Herald* (2 September 1889), p. 8.

[11] *Helena Weekly Herald* (31 October 1889), p. 8.

[12] *Helena Daily Independent* (30 May 1892), p. 1.

[13] *Helena Daily Independent* (2 January 1907), p. 5.

[14] *Helena Daily Independent* (1 February 1907), p. 1.

[15] *Ide's Helena City Directory* (1889), p. 64.

THE HOTEL DEL CORONADO
AND TENT CITY

Ann Halpenny Kantor

(1) Balloon ascension during the construction of the
     Hotel del Coronado 1887.   *San Diego Historical
     Society-Title Insurance & Trust Collection*

(2) Hotel del Coronado late 1887.   *San Diego
     Historical Society-Title Insurance & Trust Collection*

THE HOTEL DEL CORONADO
AND TENT CITY

Ann Halpenny Kantor

HE CONTRAST BETWEEN VACATIONS for the wealthy and those of more modest means can be seen in the two resorts developed by the Coronado Beach Company of California. The Hotel del Coronado, and the Tent City adjacent to it, were opened within twelve years of each other but served a very different clientele. Both were a product of railroad promotion and relied on the late Victorian faith in climate as a cure-all to attract visitors.

In 1885, the transcontinental railroad finally reached San Diego, and with it came the great real estate boom. In 1870 the population was only 2,300. At the height of the boom in early 1888 it had reached 40,000. Literally hundreds of people were arriving each month, and it was impossible to build houses and hotels fast enough for them.[1] The boom was responsible for the Hotel del Coronado, and the hotel remains a lasting symbol of the enthusiasm, extravagance, and, above all, the optimism of that fantastic period.

Directly opposite San Diego, separating San Diego Bay from the Pacific Ocean, was a narrow, uninhabited peninsula, barren except for chaparral, rabbits and quail. Two midwesterners, Elisha Babcock and H. L. Story, who had moved to San Diego for their health, often rowed across the bay to hunt rabbits. In 1885, convinced that the boom was just beginning, Babcock and Story bought the whole peninsula for $110,000. Soon after they formed a syndicate bringing in four other partners. They incorporated under the name "Coronado Beach Company," giving the peninsula a new name. Soon the land was surveyed and subdivided. Then a prospectus was prepared promising, among other things, "the largest hotel in the world ... too gorgeous to be true."[2]

In 1886 Story bought a ferryboat and organized the San Diego-Coronado Ferry Company to carry potential buyers. Passenger and freight wharves were then built and the San Diego Street Car Company was organized. The next year a railroad, the Coronado Belt Line, was built to run from San Diego, south around the bay, to Coronado. Babcock formed the Coronado Gas and Electric Company, later consolidated with companies in San Diego.[3]

The next problem was water. Babcock and Story promptly founded the Coronado Beach Water Company and pumped water from large wells sunk in the quick sands of the San Diego river under the bay to Coronado. Low rates were promised.[4]

With Barnum-like salesmanship the partners prepared for the land auctions. There were to be balloon ascensions and free tickets on the ferry and the street railway. Free water for a year was promised.[5]   (*Figure 1*)

The prospectus emphasized the wonderful climate and, as did later advertising for the hotel, made extravagant claims for its medicinal properties:

Concerning Hay Fever: It is an unquestioned fact that the climate of Coronado Beach does not merely *relieve* the sufferer from hay fever but absolutely removes every vestige of the disease. Here we fear neither Hay Fever nor Malaria, even Phthisis (tuberculosis) so prevalent and fatal in most localities, finds few victims here.[6]

The first land auction was held in November 1886, and six thousand people came across the bay to buy, sell and resell. Within a few months the auctions had brought in a million dollars, which Babcock thought would be more than enough to build his hotel.

Twenty acres in the southwest corner of Coronado had been set aside for the hotel. Late in 1886, Babcock brought architects James and Merritt Reid from Indiana where they had been employed by the David Mackey system of railroads. In an essay written fifty years later, James Reid recalled Babcock and what he wanted:

It would be built around a court ... a garden of tropical trees, shrubs and flowers, with pleasant paths . . . balconies should look down on this court from every story. From the south end, the foyer should open to Glorietta Bay with verandas. . . . On the ocean corner there should be a pavilion tower, and northward along the ocean, a colonnade, terraced in grass to the beach. The dining wing should project at an angle from the southeast corner of the court and be almost detached, to give full value to the view of the ocean, bay and city.[7]

Construction was to begin immediately but there was no lumber in San Diego and no skilled labor available. Both these problems were solved in San Francisco. Exclusive rights to all lumber cut by the Dolbeer and Carson Lumber Company were obtained and the lumber was shipped rough cut and green. A planing mill, small iron works and brick kiln were constructed at the site. Good labor, but unskilled, was obtained by applying to the Chinese Seven Companies. As many as would come were welcome and the men were trained on the job. Mrs. Babcock turned the first shovel of dirt in March 1887.[8] Working only from Reid's preliminary sketches, construction began. Reid started the foundations along the North front because construction was simpler there and he felt that as the men progressed southward, their workmanship would gradually improve. Among the problems Reid mentions were "trusses carrying heavy loads were to be constructed of green lumber and the fear of shrinking, causing settlement was present—progress was constantly hampered for want of competent men." Incandescent lighting was new and with the exception of one installation in New York, the del Coronado was the largest yet attempted. Fixtures installed were combination gas and electric, but gas was never needed.[9]

By January 1888 guests were arriving even though the hotel was not completed. Eighty freight cars brought the specially made furniture and and furnishings to the hotel. The operating staff, 324 people, were brought in from the East by special train. Extravagant advertising had been sent all over the country and with great fanfare, the official opening was held on 19 February 1888. Rooms were three dollars a day and up.[10]

The hotel was a multi-storied structure of wood with pitched shingle roof (over two million shingles were required) on which were numerous turrets, cupolas and chimneys. It covered 7½ acres and, as Babcock ordered, was built around a large quadrangle (150 x 250 feet) lighted at night with 2,000 colored lights. The view around the hotel was unobstructed—the ocean and Point Loma on the west, the bay and across the City of San Diego to the mountains on the east, and Mexico to the south. Generally the shape of the hotel was a parallelogram with two projecting corners on the front— the circular ballroom and theatre on the southwest corner and the dining room on the southeast.[11] (Figure 2)

Each of the four fronts had a wide veranda extending the entire length. The side facing the ocean was enclosed in glass, and of course, all were equipped with rocking chairs.

The front entrance to the hotel was through a large archway leading to a rotunda (lobby) sixty feet square and two stories high. Ceiling, wall and main staircase were all of Illinois Oak. A gallery running completely around the rotunda at the second level was a popular meeting place for the ladies. A gilded, cast-iron, open work elevator and a large fireplace twenty-two feet wide were notable features of the lobby. An 1890 souvenir booklet emphasizes that while the gentleman's entrance led directly into the rotunda, the ladies were ushered into a separate reception room seventy-five feet away.

Apparently the tiled floor of the rotunda went uncarpeted until 1900 and sportsmen returning from a day's outing would throw their fish and bags of game on the floor. This may explain why the ladies met in the balcony. Or perhaps they just wanted to watch all the action.

To the right of the rotunda in the southeast corner projection was the 62 x 156 foot dining room. Called the Crown Room because of its shape, this was Reid's special pride. Walls and ceiling were panelled in sugar pine. There were two huge fireplaces and windows extending nearly to the ceiling. The thirty-three foot high, arched ceiling was put together with pegs (not one nail was used), and was constructed so that there was not a single pillar nor post in the room. The tables, chairs and six large sideboards were all of oak. The Crown Room could accommodate 1,000 people and an orchestra played during dinner. (Figure 3) Both the dining room and the large breakfast room adjoining remain in use today, much as they were in 1888.

North of the Crown Room were four private dining rooms facing east, a nurses' and children's dining room, and an open-air cafe facing the courtyard. No one ever went hungry while staying at the hotel—there were three more small restaurants on the ground floor facing the ocean.

The kitchen was on the east side of the Crown Room. A large room, fifty by seventy feet, it was fitted with every modern convenience. There were also dish pantries, fruit pantries and a carving room, while directly below the kitchen were the bakery and pastry rooms.

To the left of the rotunda was the main hall, twelve feet wide and eighty feet long, with a series of public rooms opening off it on either side. There were reading, writing, smoking and chess rooms, a parlor and a music room. (Figure 4) All had fire places and were panelled in mahogany or oak with upholstery and draperies

(3) Crown Dining Room, Hotel del Coronado 1889.
San Diego Historical Society-Title Insurance &
Trust Collection

(4) Parlour, Hotel del Coronado, exact date unknown.
San Diego Historical Society-Title Insurance &
Trust Collection

in silk. The ladies billiard room was on this floor next to the ladies reception room. At the southwest corner was the ballroom-theatre projecting out from the building. A twenty foot wide promenade encircled the dance floor. The large stage was used for concerts given two or three nights a week. The Pavilion Tower which supported the walls and ceiling of the Grand Ballroom had to be incredibly strong to support the water tanks stored in the top of the tower for the gravity flow sprinkler system.

On the ground floor/basement were billiard rooms, card rooms, four bowling alleys, Turkish baths, shops and store rooms. Two giant cisterns with concrete walls, meant to store rain water but never used, were a curiosity. The hotel, then as now, had its own upholstery, furniture, electric, plumbing and machine shops, as well as its own laundry.

All guest rooms were reached from the central courtyard. There were no halls, just the outside corridors on the court yard and verandas on the upper floors. (*Figure 5*) Each suite of four of five rooms was grouped around a special reception or sitting room. There were seventy-five of these. Almost every room had a fireplace and every bedroom had its own wall safe. Originally there were seventy-three bathrooms for the 400 bedrooms.

The guest rooms were furnished in the latest and most elegant style. There were Venetian blinds and curtains of "coin dot Swiss" with fringes and cord to match the color of the dot. Each floor had its own color scheme. There was a center table in each room covered with a scarf on which was a silver tray holding a bottle of "frozen water" and two cut glass tumblers. All glassware was cut glass made in Belgium. Linens were from Scotland and toilet sets in pink, blue or brown, were made to order in England. The hotel china was Limoges with a gold crown on a white background and is still in existence.

The Hotel del Coronado was a year round resort selling health and climate so all sorts of activities were offered to keep or make the guests physically fit. There were sailboats at the boat house for the use of the guests. One could swim in the surf, in the bathhouse or the plunge. There was golf and tennis, driving or walking along the beach, archery, fishing, hunting quail or the twice weekly rabbit hunts. (*Figure 6*) For the less energetic there were concerts, card parties, sightseeing trips in the Tally-ho, the "original" Ostrich farm, the Japanese Tea Garden and, of course, all those rocking chairs.[12]

For those trying to regain their health, there were the medicinal properties of Coronado Mineral Water. Carbonated and bottled on the premises, it came right

(6)   Guests pose with a catch of sea bass outside the entrance to the Hotel del Coronado, December 1905. *San Diego Historical Society-Title Insurance & Trust Collection*

from the wells in Old Town. The Coronado Beach Company brochure assured readers that it was the only water used at the hotel and that it has an amazingly quick curative action on the functions of the liver and kindneys, it strengthens the system and beautifies the complexion.[13]

Babcock and Story had done a magnificent job of advertising their hotel. The famous and the wealthy came, stayed and returned home to spread the word. But the hotel was in serious trouble. It was still not completed and the land boom collapsed after only eighteen months. People were leaving town as quickly as possible; selling out if they could, but leaving regardless. Within a few months in 1888, the population of San Diego had dropped again—to 16,000.[14]

Fortunately, one of the wealthiest guests of the hotel came to the rescue. John D. Spreckels, son of the Spreckels sugar family, loaned Babcock $100,000 to finish the hotel. Within a few years, Spreckels owned the hotel.[15]

While a luxury hotel was a must for the wealthy, sophisticated visitor who came to Coronado, the hotel management recognized that many people of modest means were attracted to the beauty and mild summer climate of Coronado. In November 1899, the Coronado Beach Company and the Santa Fe Railroad announced plans for a Tent City to open in June 1900 on the sands south of the hotel.

---

(7)   The Tent City, Coronado 1904. Hotel del Coronado is in the background. *San Diego Historical Society-Title Insurance & Trust Collection*

(5) Interior Court of Hotel del Coronado 1890 showing
outside corridors and verandas. *San Diego
Historical Society-Title Insurance & Trust Collection*

(8) **Children's bull fight in the Plaza at the Tent City, Coronado 1905.** *San Diego Historical Society-Title Insurance & Trust Collection*

Throughout the winter and spring of 1900, the San Diego Union reported on the progress being made. A new pier was built. A. W. Swandfelt of the Los Angeles Tent and Awning Company was to provide the tents. Space would be provided for those who wished to bring their own tents. The Santa Fe Railroad announced that special trains were to run from Los Angeles, San Bernardino and Riverside direct for Tent City.

Open from June through September Tent City caught on immediately as an inexpensive, family-oriented summer resort patronized mostly by San Diegans. Outsiders came as well to escape the heat of such places as Arizona, New Mexico and Texas.[16]

Tent City was built on the sands of the strand which connected Coronado to San Diego. The camp itself was a mile long, fronting both the bay and the ocean at a place where the strand was only about 600 feet wide. (*Figure 7*)

Tents were of all sizes. Some had thatched roofs and these were interspersed with cottages. A furnished tent cost 50¢ per day for one, while a family of four could stay for a month for only thirty dollars. Cottages rented for thirty-five dollars a month. A hotel, the Arcade, provided rooms for those who wanted more comfort. The Plaza in the center of camp offered stores, restaurants, cafe, pavilion, library, reading room, merry-go-round, swings and many other attractions. (*Figure 8*)

The Tent City Band gave nightly concerts and once a week offered an afternoon of classical music. The band also doubled as an orchestra for dances. The ferry Silvergate was converted into a dance pavilion.

Health was still a major concern and every kind of outdoor sport was offered to keep guests physically fit. A variety of bathing facilities were available—surf or calm waters of the bay, cold and warm salt water plunges and an open children's pool. It is interesting to note that in 1903, instead of promising a cure, the management advertised that "consumptives" were excluded from the camp.

Tents were sparsely furnished with bare floors, only a curtain for privacy and a wash stand and pitcher for water. (*Figure 9*) Ice water was supplied free to all campers and the morning papers and twice daily mail were delivered right to the tent.

As the management put it, "Those who desire the luxuries of a grand hotel will find at the Hotel del Coronado a hearty welcome." At Tent City were those "who from choice prefer camp life ... because of its novelty, its freedom and its attractions."

Occasionally guests from the hotel came to a camp concert, while guests of tent city might wander into the lobby of the hotel, admire the Crown Room, or rock on the veranda. Guests from both resorts enjoyed the grounds and gardens of the hotel.

94

(9) Interior of Tent, Tent City, Coronado, date
unknown. *San Diego Historical Society-Title
Insurance & Trust Collection*

Here were two worlds, face to face, each enjoying the other from
a distance, and presumably, without much envy.[17]

Tent City slowly declined as the popularity of the
automobile increased, and by 1940 it was no longer a
summer resort. The Hotel del Coronado, a National
Historic Landmark, is still a luxury hotel. The verandas
and the rocking chairs are gone, as are many of the
public rooms. The rotunda is more elegant than it was
in 1888, and the Crown Room is just as impressive.
Conventions arrive now, rather than robber barons in
private railroad cars, and the boathouse is a restaurant. The Grand Ballroom still hosts magnificent balls,
but the view is somewhat obstructed by the hotel's an-
nex, Ocean Towers, to the south. Movie companies
come here as they have since 1916 and so do the great
and near great as have eight presidents and the Prince
of Wales.

NOTES

[1] E. C. MacPhail; *Story of New San Diego and of Its Founder,
Alonzo E. Horton*; Second Edition, Rev. (San Diego Historical
Society, 1979), p. 73.

[2] MacPhail, p. 74.

[3] MacPhail, p. 75.

[4] Prospectus of the Coronado Beach Company (Chicago: Rand,
McNally and Co., 1888).

[5] Marcie Buckley; *The Crown City's Brightest Gem* (Coronado,
March 1975).

[6] Prospectus of the Coronado Beach Company (1888).

[7] James W. Reid; "The Building of Hotel del Coronado"; a narrative written to commemorate the 50th anniversary of the hotel
(Coronado, 1938), pp. 2–3.

[8] Reid, pp. 4–5.

[9] Reid, pp. 5–6.

[10] Buckley, p. 14.

[11] Interior descriptions of the Hotel del Coronado 1888–1900
throughout are taken from: *Souvenir of the Hotel del Coronado*
(1890); *Album of San Diego and Coronado Beach* (Columbus,
Ohio: Ward Brothers, January 1889); Buckley, pp. 31–33.

[12] Burke Ormsby; "The Lady Who Lives By The Sea"; *Journal
of San Diego History*, Vol. XII, no. 1 (San Diego Historical
Society, January 1966).

[13] Coronado Beach Company (1888).

[14] MacPhail, p. 95.

[15] Ormsby, p. 12.

[16] Descriptions of Tent City throughout are taken from: Mac-
Phail, pp. 125–126; Tent City Prospectus (1903, 1904, 1920).

[17] MacPhail, p. 126.

MEET ME IN DREAMLAND: THE EARLY DEVELOPMENT OF AMUSEMENT PARKS IN AMERICA

Richard W. Flint

MEET ME IN DREAMLAND:
THE EARLY DEVELOPMENT OF
AMUSEMENT PARKS IN AMERICA

Richard W. Flint

IN THE EARLY PART OF THIS CENTURY nearly every American city had its amusement park. To enter such a park was to be transported into an illusionary world of fantasy complete with bizarre architecture, exotic shows, and thrilling rides. Conceived and designed as one entity much like today's theme parks, the first amusement parks had their antecedents in several resort hotel areas which sought to extend their popularity and business by adding a few mechanical amusement rides.

There were many basic changes occurring in the American way of life that set the stage for the emergence of the amusement park and which, historically, made it a cultural symbol of the rising, new American lifestyle. Life in nineteenth-century America was in many ways more "Victorian" than the England ruled by Queen Victoria. Genteel culture arbitrated public taste but by the end of the century impatience with the old restraints surfaced among a new generation of Americans, the urban working class. Leisure, once spent in edifying activities of moral and social value, was now the new market for entrepreneurs who found a swelling urban population with increased time and spending power.

The most striking expression of this change was in the new amusement parks which were developing as the Victorian age ended. Earlier public parks had sought to provide a contemplative rural retreat but the developing commercial parks were called amusement parks because they aimed to amuse rather than to uplift. Here were the mechanical amusements in an industrial age with which the visitor could associate. Here, too, were grandiose and exotic settings from which he could escape his drab world. No longer was he the spectator but rather an intimate participant in the spectacle about him. Now the pleasure seeker was the actor upon the stage.

The amusement parks which developed at the turn of the century can tell us much about the change from a genteel, rural culture to an urban, industrial age. Americans did not seek to escape the raucousness of the new age for they went to the amusement park where they found a familiar setting of crowds, mechanical wonders, and rapidly changing experiences. If they escaped to anything, it was to an exotic world but not a foreign one. Many had fled the poor rural life for the promise of the city and though they might not yet have realized their dream, they could find it for a day at an amusement park .

The ancestor of the amusement park is the urban pleasure garden such as those which began flourishing in eighteenth-century London—Vauxhall, Ranelagh, Marylebone, and Sadler's Wells, for example. In a pastoral setting and amid ornamented pathways, people of all classes could find liquid refreshments, music, and outdoor performances by a wide variety of entertainers. In America, similar privately owned pleasure gardens were established in New York, Boston, Baltimore, and Charlestown. In Philadelphia, Vauxhall Gardens opened in 1814 and even took its name from London's most famous pleasure retreat. Beer, soda water, and ice creams could be had amidst music, gas lights, theatrical events, and sometimes fireworks or balloon ascensions. In its short eleven year existence, the architecture of Philadelphia's Vauxhall evolved from Moorish in 1814 to Chinese and then to French, the last occasioned by Lafayette's visit in 1825.[1]

Not only is a sufficient population center needed to economically support a regular entertainment company, but there must also be a sufficient amount of time, money, and cultural approval for people to indulge in leisure activities. Following the Civil War, all such criteria were met in this country and many new entrepreneurs quickly arose to satisfy the thirst for amuse-

(2) Part of a panoramic view of Rochester, New York, showing the resorts along Lake Ontario and Irondequoit Bay. From *Rochester's Pleasure Resorts: "How to Get There"* [Rochester, New York: Rochester Railway Co., 1901]. *Courtesy Rochester Public Library, Local History Division*

(1) A portable merry-go-round at a Nahant, Massachusetts, seaside resort. From a stereo view by Surdam & White, 305 Broadway, New York, N. Y., ca. 1870. *Author's Collection*

ment. P. T. Barnum personifies the most brazen and successful example but there were others who capitalized on leisure pursuits: resort operators, the railroad magnates who provided the transportation to the resorts, and the brewers who made the liquid refreshments sold at the resorts, among many others.

The development of many outdoor resorts was a profitable answer to the appeal that nature has long had for man. The salt air and sublime vistas attracted a few wealthy visitors to Coney Island but when public transportation reached the area in the 1850s, middle and working classes began to come and bath houses and boarding houses sprang up. Elsewhere, on the Jersey coast, speculators bought land, built a railroad to the new Atlantic City in the 1850s, and then saw the value of their land rise as working-class Philadelphians bought train tickets to vacation at the burgeoning resort.[2]

Atlantic City, Coney Island, and the amusement area known as the Midway Plaisance at the 1893 World's Columbian Exposition in Chicago have all been given credit for the fostering of the modern amusement park. In many ways, however, they were merely the largest and best known and what was evolving at Coney Island was occuring at countless other, smaller resorts throughout the country. Atlantic City had a mechanical pleasure wheel (or Ferris wheel as it is now called) by 1872 and Coney Islanders were riding a merry-go-round in the 1870s.[3] Such mechanical rides date back centuries and the first recorded appearance of a merry-go-round in this country is in Salem, Massachusetts, in 1800. About 1830, the residents of Market Street Slip petitioned New York City official Gideon Lee to permit Joshua Taylor to continue to operate his merry-go-round described as "four automoton figures or horses upon a machine by which to move round a circle."[4] By the late 1870s, manufacturer John J. Wagoner & Co. of Cincinnati frequently advertised their "Parisian Carrousells" for sale in the New York Clipper, an amusement trade journal. Showmen would travel from place to place with the small and sometimes crude carousels and set up their portable machines for a few weeks wherever there were crowds of people with some leisure time. (Figure 1) Most such locations were at county fairs or local resorts where visitors sought recreation when away from work or household chores.

The evolution of some earlier amusement parks is exemplified by Rochester, New York, and its several resorts. (Figure 2) Rochester sits on the Genesee River, about six miles south of Lake Ontario. Located at the mouth of the Genesee on the lake is the town of Charlotte; a few miles east on the lakefront is Irondequoit Bay.

The development of outdoor sports marked a significant change in Victorian social life. With increased boating and fishing on Irondequoit Bay, Newport House, the first local summer hotel, opened in 1856. When lake bathing appeared in the 1850s, Martin McIntyre, the operator of a fisherman's lodge or "pier saloon" in Charlotte, announced that dressing tents were available on the shore in front of his establishment. Fishing and boating, however, remained the principal attractions as summer camps and cottages began to dot both Charlotte and Irondequoit Bay in the 1860s and 1870s. In 1873 the 76 room Spencer House replaced McIntyre's old lodge and the next year Charlotte became the leading resort with the construction of the Cottage Hotel and four smaller hotels. Several miles east of Charlotte, at Irondequoit Bay, the Sea Breeze House faced Lake Ontario. In July 1879 the Rochester and Lake Ontario Railroad reached Sea Breeze and so spurred rival Charlotte to improve its transport lines with the city of Rochester ten miles to the south. When in 1883 the Lake Ontario Beach Improvement Company acquired twenty acres at Charlotte Beach and opened the expansive new Hotel Ontario the next year, the railroad looped its track through the grounds to facilitate excursion trains. Excursion steamers like the commodious "Flower City," equipped to take 700 passengers, provided the most pleasant journey

from Irondequoit Bay and Charlotte and other points on the lake. As the important transportation network with Rochester expanded, other small resort communities emerged along the lake such as Summerville and White City, the latter so named because of its neat rows of white tents set on board floors. The resort communities housed city families for the summer while those employed in the city would commute on the rail lines.[5]

Charlotte and Irondequoit Bay housed some of the principal summer resorts among several which a Rochester newspaper called "a paradise for poor people." "Amid all the heat and bustle of the city," wrote a reporter in 1894, "Rochester can proudly boast of possessing a greater number of inviting, convenient, and accessible 'outing spots' than any city in the country. No one need run away from town for rest, for right here at our doors are many cool retreats richly blessed in beauty and scenery." Acknowledging the severe impact of the Panic of 1893, the reporter continued: "An important feature of an outing in these hard times lies in the question of cost . . . and enjoyable recreation can be so secured by a sojourn at home." The reporter then went on to describe nineteen "charming resorts near at hand."[6]

Of the many "charming resorts," it would be some of the larger hotels which would eventually spawn mechanical amusement rides and then emerge into modern amusement parks.

Undoubtedly, itinerant showmen appeared at Rochester's resorts before the newspapers or other sources bothered to mention them incidently. A "dummy circus on a large scale" which, thankfully, the reporter went on to explain was a merry-go-round "propelled by a small steam engine," appeared under a tent at Sea Breeze in 1883.[7]

The second merry-go-round known to have been in Rochester was operated by a Philadelphia family which would later have long connections with Rochester's amusement parks. Arthur and George Long, two brothers, were operating a merry-go-round at Ontario Beach by 1892 and Arthur Long continued through 1907. His brother George left the carousel business for much of the 1890s to work as a tapestry weaver but in 1899 and 1900 operated his carousel at Cape May, New Jersey, and in 1901 and 1902 he was at Burlington Island, between Trenton and Philadelphia. The following year, 1903, George Long went to Piney Beach, outside of Norfolk, Virginia, but did very little business with his merry-go-round since the area had not been developed. From his family which operated the carousel at Rochester's Ontario Beach, George Long learned of the opportunity to put his merry-go-round at Sea Breeze on

(3)   The George Long carousel at Sea Breeze, Rochester, New York, 1904. Constructed by the Long family (with the animals carved by a Philadelphian named named Leopold [pronounced Loop-old]) in 1899, it was similar to another machine made by them about 1895-96 which replaced an earlier machine, also Long-built, at Ontario Beach. Young George Long, Jr., is standing behind the horse to the right of center; his father, George, Sr., is further right near the horse's head.   Courtesy George W. Long, Jr., and Sea Breeze Amusement Park, Rochester, NY

Irondequoit Bay in 1904.[8] (Figure 3) Today, his great-grandchildren manage the park that is still at Sea Breeze.

In 1883, before the tenure of the Long family, Sea Breeze, with its "dummy circus," or merry-go-round, was called "Rochester's Coney Island." "It was like a Fourth of July at the Sea Breeze yesterday afternoon," said a reporter. "By far the quietest place there being the old hotel which bears that name and gives a popular name to the locality. The surroundings were extremely festive." He went on to note that a brass band entertained at one beer garden while another party danced a quadrille to the tune of a violin and banjo. A Punch and Judy show and shooting galleries provided entertainment in clamourous competition to numerous swings and a bowling alley. Picnicers were present as was the omni-present odor of broiling sausages. The newspaperman then observed that

considering the vast and heterogeneous crowd that visits the lake and bay resorts on Sunday it is a wonder that they behave as well as they do . . . The element of semi-intoxication is ever present to invite disturbance, and competitive games lend their influence to provide contention and discord.[9]

Ten years later the same newspaper noted that "the Sea Breeze, as a summer resort, has, during recent years, attracted patronage of not the most orderly or desireable character." [10] In 1896, for example, a woman was killed

by the accidental discharge of a gun at a shooting gallery near a gambling wheel and the result was a temporary enforcement of a Sunday law against shooting galleries and gambling devices.[11] By 1900, however, the Sea Breeze area was tranquil enough for the local YMCA chapter to open a vacation home for young women.[12] In 1903, the first permanent, large-scale amusement ride was installed, a roller coaster, and the next year George Long and his merry-go-round arrived. The independent concessionaires leased space from the railway company which owned the land and eventually George Long, Jr., would acquire the entire park in 1946.[13]

The roller coaster, a relatively tame affair in which the cars slowly descended three levels of track, each shaped like a figure–8, was not the first permanent ride in Rochester. At least four different rides were installed at Ontario Beach in Charlotte and the Summerville shore had a water slide in flat-bottomed boats, the type of ride that would be the focal point of many coming amusement parks.

(4)   The Paul Boyton chute at Summerville, Rochester, New York. Photograph, ca. 1890s.   Courtesy Department of Rare Books, Manuscripts, and Archives, University of Rochester

The Paul Boyton chute (Figure 4) was named for a remarkable Victorian popular hero, now largely forgotten. While in the lifesaving service at Atlantic City in 1874, Capt. Boyton learned of a rubber suit with air pockets that would keep a man afloat. Boyton practiced daily with a two-bladed paddle and then in the fall of 1874 he announced he would board a ship and when 200 miles offshore, swim home. His attempt was thwarted by a worried sea captain until convinced by Boyton to be allowed to try the stunt off the Irish shore. He garnered great publicity and then toured for many years with a water show and often swam great distances along famous rivers. He arrived at Coney Island in 1895 to open Sea Lion Park which featured a number of aquatic attractions including forty performing sea lions, hence the park's name. The park was enclosed and charged an admission price. Once inside, other attractions, including a chute, were available. Sea Lion Park, because it was enclosed and charged an admission price, is credited with being the first modern amusement park.[14] Boyton, however, apparently marketed the chutes in other cities, including Rochester, a town in which he had performed his water stunts during the summer of 1882.[15] A Rochesterian described a ride in the locally famous chute in 1899:

We get into the car and are taken up a steep incline to the top of a lofty tower. There are other inclines, but they are fitted with rollers, and the car is a four-seated affair like a flat-bottomed boat. We take our seats in this and say "yes" to the "are you ready" of the gondolier, when—zipp! rumble!! splash!!! we are down to the bottom, our vehicle floating about in the waters of the large basin below. Oh! but that was exhilarating, even if it did take our breath away, and we are not wet with even so much as one drop of water.[16]

Adjacent to Boyton's chute in Summerville was a huge electric fountain which, the same writer explained, "throws several gracefully drooping streams which, at night, are illuminated by variously hued rays of light which are projected upon them from some unseen source, producing a beautiful and dazzling effect."

Of all the summer places near Rochester, Charlotte was the largest and most popular. Like Sea Breeze, it was termed in 1891 "the 'Coney Island' of Western New York" and by 1906 was acknowledged as "Rochester's great summer resort for the masses" with "a continual round of entertainment in the shape of vaudeville shows and popular and spectacular out-door attractions" as well as concerts "afternoons and evenings by bands of national repute."[17]

A broad avenue reaching north to the beach at Charlotte had several small hotels but the two major resorts flanked either side of the avenue and faced the beach. The older of the two was on the west side and was constructed in 1874 as the Cottage Hotel. (Figure 5) In the 1880s the Cottage was acquired by Rochester's major brewery, the Bartholomay Brewing Company. Some 350 carriages could be accommodated and the entire grounds were lighted by electricity supplied by a dynamo in the hotel's engine house which also pumped water from the lake. A brochure explained that

The hotel consists of a number of handsome cottages in the Swiss style of architecture, surrounded by a beautiful veranda sixteen feet wide and about a quarter of a mile in length. It contains elegant dining rooms and parlors, billiard rooms, and in fact everything requisite in a first-class hotel. . . . Near the hotel stands the large pavilion, accommodating 5,000 people. Here the

large excursions, visiting the beach almost daily during the season, make their headquarters, and the famous product of the Bartholomay Brewing Company is dispensed . . .[18]

On the east side of the avenue facing the lake was the rival Hotel Ontario, built in 1884. A wide boardwalk, emulating Asbury Park, fronted the lake and between it and the hotel was the esplanade with its beds of flowers, a bandstand, and a bath house. The bathing house, in 1894, featured an "entire new outfitting of first-class bathing suits . . . and for 25 cents one can enjoy a delightfully cool bath in new and cleanly suits. Safe-lockers are provided for valuables and . . . abundance of towels and all convenient accessories are generously provided."[19] In addition, the bathing pavilion featured a toboggan slide, "where bathers congregate to enjoy the exhilarating and wildly mirthful pleasure of a sliding plunge into the waves."[20]

Extending from the hotel grounds nearly a half mile into the lake was the government pier, a popular spot for local fishermen, promenaders, and lake boats.

The Hotel Ontario itself was a three story structure and just next to it, on the east side, was the Auditorium. The first auditorium was destroyed by fire in October 1894 and the second, larger structure was built on its site the following spring. Described as being of Swiss architecture and painted a soft olive green on the outside, it featured a stage, dressing rooms, a main floor and balcony with a seating capacity of 1200, and cost about $20,000. Tables were provided for the occupants and refreshments were served in the natural pine setting of the vaudeville and concert hall.[21]

At various locations about the grounds were several mechanical amusement rides as well as concessionaires offering popcorn, candy, and ice creams. A merry-go-round was probably the first ride but positive evidence does not record one before Arthur and George Long's presence in 1892. In 1894 the local newspaper not only noted a merry-go-round but also a roller coaster, mystic swing, and maze as well as "fakirs and all the life and bustle of a modern watering place."[22] Five years later, in 1899, the list of rides was about the same but a Rochester Railway Company brochure differentiates two different roller coasters—a switchback and a "Russian railway."[23] The latter probably takes its name from an early ride called the "Russian Mountains" which operated in Paris in 1804. It was a modification for the warmer French climate of the popular Russian ice slides, modified by using rolling carriages instead of sleds to carry passengers down an inclined plane. In America, an industrial "roller coaster," actually a gravity-operated inclined coal railway, operated at Mauch Chunk, Pennsylvania, and was converted to an amusement ride in 1870. Stationary engines would pull the

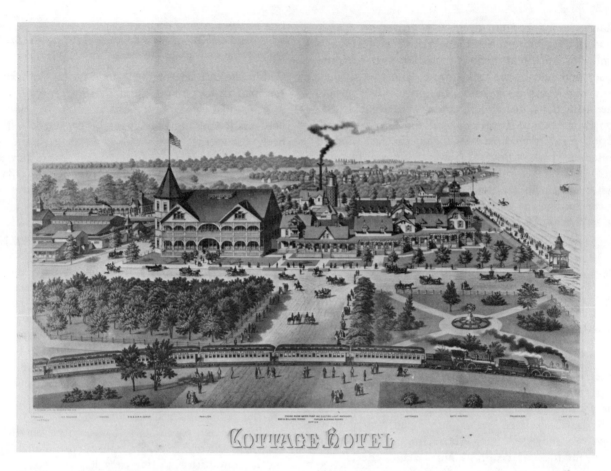

COTTAGE HOTEL

(5)   The Cottage Hotel looking east across Lake Avenue
from the grounds of the Hotel Ontario. From a
lithograph (59 1/2 x 80 cm.) by the Stecher Lith.
Co., Rochester, NY, ca. 1890.   *Courtesy
Department of Rare Books, Manuscripts, and
Archives, University of Rochester*

cars up the initial hills until gravity took over. At the
end of the line the direction of the cars was reversed or
switched, hence the name "switchback."

In 1884, LaMarcus A. Thompson patented and built
at Coney Island a "switchback railway." The 36 year
old Thompson had been a hosiery manufacturer but
health forced him to sell his business. In the next three
years he obtained thirty patents and, in 1895, incorporated his L. A. Thompson Scenic Railway Co. By
then, it was no longer necessary to switch back the cars
onto a return track halfway through the ride for other
ride developers discovered the idea of a continuous,
circular track—the "serpentine railway." Thompson
countered by providing scenery and tunnels and so developed the scenic railway. Whether his coasters were
among the first at Ontario Beach in the 1890s is not
known but after about 1906 an L. A. Thompson Scenic
Railway did operate at the amusement park. By about

the same date, the grounds of the Hotel Ontario with
its now numerous amusement rides were enclosed and
the area was no longer a resort hotel but rather had
evolved into a modern amusement park, Ontario Beach
Park.[24]   *(Figure 6)*

Like Coney Island and other resort areas, Rochester's water front hotels were popular Sunday and
vacation retreats for working Americans. The more
prosperous of these resorts, such as the Sea Breeze House
and Hotel Ontario, provided recreation in such forms
as music, vaudeville, and mechanical amusement rides.
Such evolutions did not go unnoticed.

In 1894 a group of Cleveland businessmen decided
to open an 1890s pleasure garden called Euclid Beach.
In their prospectus they said they were

convinced that a Summer Resort within easy reach of Cleveland,
properly appointed and conducted, will be both popular and
profitable ... The design is to enclose the property, lay out drives
and walks, plant and transplant trees, put in an Electrical Fountain, build a Casino, Bath and Boat Houses, Toboggan Slides and
such other attractions as may be deemed advisable.

The park opened in 1895 and by 1896 a "Switch-Back
Railway," merry-go-round, and Ferris wheel were there.[25]

The parks which developed at Rochester and Cleveland were all situated on lakefront property but even a

(6) Post card view of "Charlotte on Lake Ontario—The
Coney Island of Central New York," ca. 1906. The
reasonably accurate artist's view shows the
Auditorium (the two-story circular structure in the
center of the picture), the Hotel Ontario to the right
of the Auditorium, and the assorted amusements
including the L. A. Thompson Scenic Railway in
the lower left along Irondequoit Bay; the Lake
Ontario beach is in the lower right. The artist omits
numerous other hotels and businesses which abutted
the ground. *Author's Collection*

town as land-locked as Altoona, Pennsylvania, developed a pleasure resort. The trolley and railroad lines,
normally carrying great numbers of people only during
the work week, found profitable weekend business in
the passengers who went to parks and summer hotels.
Soon they began to develop property at the end of their
electrical lines, thus also providing lights for the grounds
and power for the new mechanical rides. In Altoona,
the stockholders of the Altoona and Logan Valley Electric Railway Company formed the Lakemont Park
Company in 1894. The new company took over a former swamp that had been excavated to form a lake and
had become a popular local picnic site. In 1894 a casino
was constructed and soon a theatre with its own acting
company was built while one Amandus Sink began to
develop the major amusements in the 1890s.[26] In 1901
the merry-go-round burned and the following year E.

Joy Morris of Philadelphia built a replacement for
$8000. For an additional $12,500 Morris constructed an
80 x 250 foot figure–8 style wooden roller coaster. Virtually all figure–8 style coasters, as well as switchbacks
and scenic railways, were replaced by faster and more
sensational coaster rides in the 1920s. However, along
with its carousel, Altoona's Lakemont Park coaster survives as the last of its breed and the oldest roller coaster
in America. Still called "Leap-the-Dips" (pronounced
locally by some as "lipitty-dips"), it deserves recognition
by preservationists and, with its dips of about four
feet, provides a feeling of what thrilled turn-of-the-
century Americans.[27]

In 1898 *Harper's Monthly* reported that "the great
recreation-grounds run by the street-railway company,
with all sorts of attractions—band concerts, variety performances, a menagerie, swings, teeter-boards, roller-
coasters, fireworks, etc. . . . are now very numerous
throughout the country." [28] In 1902, a *Cosmopolitan*
writer acknowledged that

the expression, "trolley-park," may not as yet have come into
common use, but no explanation of its meaning is necessary . . .
The fact is that the street and suburban railway companies,
realizing the profit arising by catering to the pleasure of the
masses, have entered into the amusement field on an extensive
scale . . . These parks, combining natural and artificial diversions,
have become the Mecca on holidays and Sundays not only of
what we are pleased to term the working classes but of the
"middle millions." [29]

(7) Post card "View of Glen Haven, One of Rochester's beautiful Summer Resorts," ca. 1908. The octagonal building in the center housed a merry-go-round; to the right and in the foreground are booths for games and concessions; to the left is the figure-8 roller coaster. The view shows virtually all of the amusement area of Glen Haven, later Dreamland, Park which evolved from the local resort area around the Glen Haven House, visible behind the roller coaster and facing Irondequoit Bay in the background. *Author's Collection*

Meanwhile, at Coney Island, a Ferris wheel operator named George T. Tilyou imitated Boyton's idea of an enclosed park and opened Steeplechase Park in 1897. As Tilyou observed, "we Americans want to be thrilled or amused, and we are ready to pay well for either sensation." [30] On the lookout for new attractions for his park, Tilyou visited the midway of the 1901 Pan-American Exposition in Buffalo, New York, and was captivated by a dramatic cyclorama, "A Trip to the Moon," created by Frederic Thompson and Skip Dundy. Thompson and Dundy and their attraction came to Steeplechase Park but after the 1902 season they left to create their own park. They bought Boyton's Sea Lion Park, tore down all the attractions except the shoot-the-chutes and its central lagoon, and erected the most ambitious amusement park up to that time, Luna Park, named for Dundy's sister, Luna.

A former architect's draftsman, Frederic Thompson, more than any other showman of his era, realized the entertainment potential of architecture. Abandoning all conventional standards, he created what he called "Free Renaissance" using "all the license in the world." [31] Here was the architecture of pleasure that engulfed the visitor or, in the words of Albert Bigelow Paine, "an enchanted, storybook land of trellises, columns, domes, minarets, lagoons, and lofty aerial flights. And everywhere was life—a pageant of happy people." [32]

But the 250,000 glittering lights of Luna encouraged imitators. The following year, 1904, another park, aptly named Dreamland, opened under the glare of 1,000,000 light bulbs. Other specially designed amusement parks soon opened around the country and engineers such as Pittsburgh's Frederick Ingersoll, who also named his parks Luna, specialized in their design. Many of the parks adopted the names of the famous Coney Island parks such as Rochester's trolley park, Glen Haven, which renamed itself Dreamland. (*Figure 7*) By 1909, when the hit song "Meet Me Tonight in Dreamland" sold five million copies, dreamland no longer meant some romantic place devoid of roller coasters and carousels.

NOTES

1 Harold Donaldson Eberlain and Cortlandt Van Dyke Hubbard, "The American 'Vauxhall' of the Federal Era," *Pennsylvania Magazine of History and Biography* 68 (April 1944): pp. 150–74; Joseph Jackson, "Vauxhall Garden," *Pennsylvania Magazine of History and Biography* 57 (1933): pp. 289–98; see also Thomas Myers Garrett, "A History of Pleasure Gardens in New York City, 1700–1865," Ph.D. dissertation, New York University, 1978.

2 Charles E. Funnell, *By the Beautiful Sea* (New York: Alfred A. Knopf, 1975) is the best history of Atlantic City. Robert E. Snow and David E. Wright, "Coney Island: A Case Study in Popular Culture and Technical Change," *Journal of Popular Culture* 9 (Spring 1976): pp. 960–75, and John F. Kasson's excellent interpretive study, *Amusing the Million: Coney Island at the Turn of the Century* (New York: Hill and Wang, 1978), contain references to the standard Coney Island literature.

3 Funnell, *By the Beautiful Sea*, p. 62; William Mangels, *The Outdoor Amusement Business* (New York: Vantage Press, 1952) is still the standard history of the amusement ride business and was written by one of the industry's pioneers.

4 *Salem Impartial Register* (30 June 1800); Gideon Lee papers, New York State Library, Albany.

5 Blake McKelvey, "Rochester Learns to Play: 1850–1900," *Rochester History* 8 (July 1946): p. 3; Blake McKelvey, *Rochester, The Flower City, 1855–1890* (Cambridge, Massachusetts: Harvard University Press, 1949), pp. 49, 177, 353; Rochester Railway Company, *Souvenir of Rochester: Its Attractions and Pleasure Resorts* (Rochester, New York: Post Express Printing Co., 1899), pp. 50–51.

6 "Summering in Rochester," (Rochester, New York) *Union and Advertiser* (3 July 1894), p. 10.

7 "Rochester's Coney Island," *Ibid.* (25 June 1883), p. 2.

8 Tape recorded interview with George W. Long, Jr., Rochester, New York, 2 November 1974.

9 "Rochester's Coney Island," *Union and Advertiser* (25 June 1883), p. 2.

10 "Sea Breeze Improvements," *Ibid.* (26 June 1893), p. 5.

11 "No More Games," *Ibid.* (14 July 1896), p. 2.

12 Blake McKelvey, *Rochester, the Quest for Quality, 1890–1925* (Cambridge, Massachusetts: Harvard University Press, 1956), p. 127.

13 Long interview.

14 Mangels, *Outdoor Amusement Industry*, pp. 38–40; Edo McCullough, *Good Old Coney Island* (New York: Charles Scribner's Sons, 1957), pp. 296–99.

15 *Union and Advertiser* (15 July 1882), p. 3.

16 Rochester Railway Company, *Souvenir of Rochester*, p. 49.

17 *Fourth Annual Report of the Rochester Chamber of Commerce...For the Year Ending December 31st, 1891* (Rochester, New York: Union and Advertiser, 1892), p. 22; Rochester Chamber of Commerce, *Rochester 1906* (N.p., n.d.), p. 13.

18 *Bartholomay Brewing Company, Rochester, N. Y.* (N.p., n.d.), pp. 7–8; this small souvenir booklet to advertise the summer hotel is in the collections of the Department of Rare Books, Manuscripts and Archives, University of Rochester, Rochester, New York, and can be dated after 1887.

19 "Summering in Rochester," *Union and Advertiser* (3 July 1894), p. 10.

20 Rochester Railway Company, *Souvenir of Rochester*, p. 47.

21 "New Auditorium," *Union and Advertiser* (6 April 1895), p. 10.

22 "Ontario's Shores," *Ibid.* (13 August 1894), p. 8; "Summering in Rochester," *Ibid.* (3 July 1894), p. 10.

23 Rochester Railway Company, *Souvenir of Rochester*, p. 47.

24 Thompson's obituary appears in the *New York Times* (9 March 1919), p. 20; the Thompson coaster at Ontario Beach appears in the photographic and post card collections of the Rochester Museum and Science Center, Rochester, New York.

25 Lee O. Bush, et al., *Euclid Beach Park is Closed for the Season* (Cleveland, Ohio: Dillon/Liederbach, 1977), pp. 2, 4, 9.

26 *Lakemont Park: Your Park and its History* [Altoona, Pennsylvania: Lakemont Park Citizens' Advisory Council, n.d.], *passim.*; the dates for the construction of the rides are incorrect.

27 See *Lakemont Park* [1902], an unpaged promotional brochure.

28 Sylvester Baxter, "The Trolley in Rural Parts," *Harper's Monthly* 97 (June 1898), p. 61.

29 Day Allen Willey, "The Trolley-Park," *Cosmopolitan* 33 (July 1902), pp. 265, 267–70.

30 Reginald Wright Kauffman, "Why is Coney?" *Hampton's Magazine* 23 (August 1909), p. 224.

31 Frederic Thompson, "Amusing the Million," *Everybody's Magazine* 19 (September 1908), p. 385; biographical information on Frederic Thompson, who was no relation to LaMarcus Adna Thompson, appears in Oliver Pilat and Jo Ranson, *Sodom by the Sea* (Garden City, New York: Doubleday, Doran, 1941), pp. 142 ff., and Robert Grau, *The Business Man in the Amusement World* (New York: Broadway Publishing Co., 1910), pp. 328–29.

32 "The New Coney Island," *Century* 68 (August 1904), p. 535.

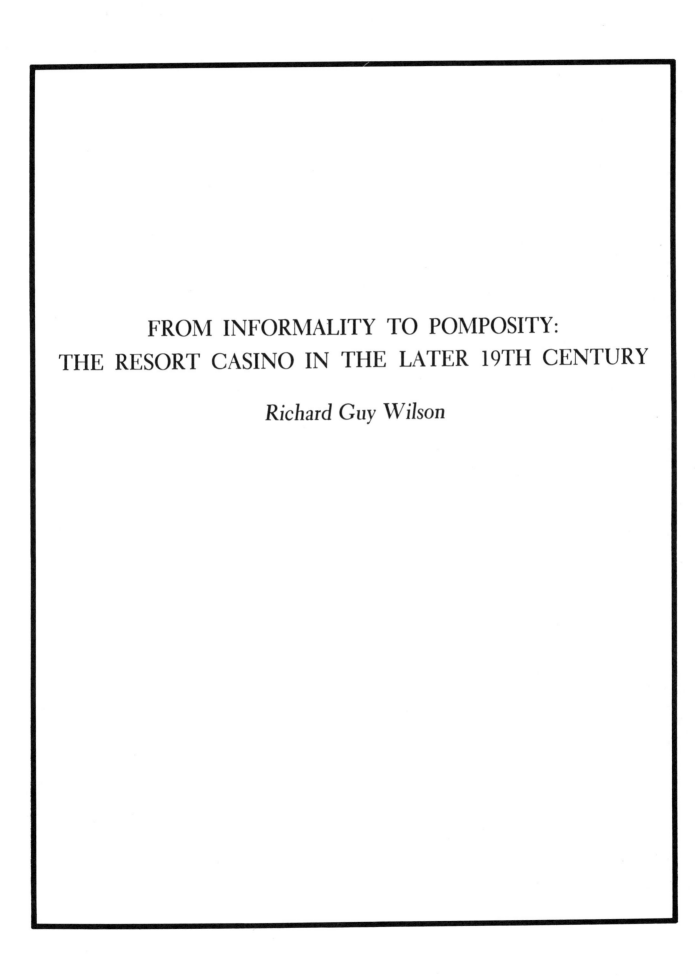

FROM INFORMALITY TO POMPOSITY:
THE RESORT CASINO IN THE LATER 19TH CENTURY

Richard Guy Wilson

FROM INFORMALITY TO POMPOSITY:
THE RESORT CASINO IN THE LATER 19TH CENTURY

Richard Guy Wilson

IN THE PERIOD 1876–1910, the "casino" or the "country clubhouse" appeared on the American resort scene and became a focal point for social activities. The evolution of this building type from thin wooden pavilions nearly as ephemeral as the shifting sand, as in J. P. Putnam's Casino at Nahant, to pretentious Georgian halls, as in McKim, Mead & White's Stockbridge Casino, illustrates both changing architectural tastes and new attempts at social stratification. (Figures 1 and 2)

The origin of the word "casino" is Italian and means a small summer house, or alternatively a building or pavilion designed for pleasure and located in a garden.[1] By the later 18th and early 19th century, the word casino appears in English and French, but associated with a slightly different building type. For the French and English, "casino" came to mean rooms or a clubhouse used for social occasions: dancing, music or the theater, and located at a spa. The Casino at Monte Carlo remains the most famous or infamous out of the literally hundreds that dotted European watering spots in the 19th century. Functionally, the American casino owed a great deal to these European prototypes, but with one significant exception: gambling seldom made an appearance in the American resort casino.[2] (The association of the casino with gambling is much more a twentieth century phenomenon.) The debt in function to the European casino by the American casino does not carry through in architectural image; the American casino became a unique building type in its own right.

The identification of the first American casino is unclear (possibly it is Putnam's at Nahant),[3] but certainly one of the earliest and the best known is the Newport Casino of 1879–1880 by the New York architectural firm of McKim, Mead & White. Of those concerned with the design of casinos, McKim, Mead &

White were certainly the most important; they created the wellknown examples at Newport, Narragansett, Short Hills and Stockbridge, giving form and definition to the building type. Later, they helped to alter the concept of the casino as in their work for the Astor family at Rhinebeck. Consequently, the role of McKim, Mead & White in the development of the American casino will be stressed.

Of the three partners, Charles F. McKim (1847–1909) led the way in defining the architecture the office would produce. Educated at the Ecole des Beaux Arts in Paris in the late 1860s and then in H. H. Richardson's office for a few years in the early 1870s, he had by 1879 an established reputation as an architect of resort and country houses.[4] William R. Mead (1846–1928), the second partner, served as the office manager and engineer; he brought the sometimes wild and impractical designs of his partners down to earth. The third partner, Stanford White (1853–1906), best known for his flamboyant night life in New York City, and his departure from that life, was known as a gifted draftsman and ornamentalist. As a designer, White was clearly McKim's subordinate, though his light and free touch frequently relieved McKim's more ponderous hand. The Newport Casino was McKim, Mead & White's first major commission. It entered the office within a few days of White's own entry on 8 September 1879.

By the later 1870s, Newport had already attained a position of preeminence as a resort for wealthy society. A casino had been proposed for Newport in 1878,[5] but it was not until 1879 that the idea became a reality through the actions of James Gordon Bennett, Jr. James Gordon Bennett, Jr., the owner of the *New York Herald*, was a wealthy young man with a predisposition to wild, impetuous and generally intoxicated behavior. Accepted into New York society for his wealth but

(1) The Casino at Nahant, Mass. J. P. Putnam, architect. The New York Sketch Book of Architecture, 1876

(2) The Newport Casino, Newport, R. I., McKim, Mead & White, architects. *Library of Congress, Detroit Photographic Company*

with unease because of his behavior, Bennett had caused a major scandal in early 1879 by urinating in front of his fiancée in a fireplace.[6] His engagement broken, and ostracized from polite company, he determined to create still another scandal and show the thin veneer of genteel manners that overly society's baser instincts for scandal, fun and entertainment. A visiting British Army officer friend accepted a challenge to ride a horse inside the old, prestigious and staid Newport Reading room; an action that caused the friend's expulsion and allowed Bennett to issue a challenge. A few days later, the Newport *Mercury* reported that Bennett had purchased a site on Bellevue Avenue across from his own home for a "new club house," and the further "Mr. Bennett has been led to take this step by reason of the dismissal of a friend from the Newport Reading Room for a clear violation of the rules of that institution."[7] Bennett founded a limited stock company and a short time later Charles McKim arrived in Newport to inspect the site and discuss plans.[8] Construction began in January 1880, and by July, the doors were opened to the public, although the grounds were not finished until the summer of 1881. The casino contained conversation and lounging rooms, a restaurant, a billiard room, a theater, piazzas for strolling, and tennis courts.[9] In 1881, the first National Lawn Tennis Tournament was held at the casino. Exclusive in the sense that membership was required for entry, any person with the necessary money could join for periods varying from a week to a season. However, there were carefully delineated boundaries and the casino became known for its exclusiveness. Perhaps the most notorious case was the snubbing of

President Chester A. Arthur as a person of no social consequence by doormen who forced him to call his own carriage.[10] Having proved his point that society would follow entertainment rather than decorum, Bennett sold his share in the casino in 1881 at a profit.

The building by McKim, Mead & White fronted on Bellevue Avenue with stores located on the ground floor and entertainment spaces on the second and third floors. A large central entrance arch gave access to the upper floors and also the horseshoe court and tennis pavilions in the rear. Next door stood Richard Morris Hunt's slightly earlier (1875) Travers Block which in its restless agitation contrasted with the calm coolness and order of McKim's design. The casino front was described by a critic as "an extremely beautiful adaptation of Early and Modern English," an indication of the origins of the design in the contemporary work of Richard Norman Shaw's Queen Anne.[11] McKim adopted certain Queen Anne features but greatly simplified them. Three reiterated cross gables cap the long horizontal sweep of the lower floors. The voids of the ground level (framed by brick piers) stand in contrast to the overhanging volumetric billowing of the shingled second floor. Five different shaped shingles catch the sun and create impressionistic display. The cut wood reliefs in the gables, the cornice and frieze with sunflowers are avowedly Queen Anne, and the central porch is a creative gloss on a Palladian window.

The upstairs interior is much altered and only a few fireplace mantels give testimony to Stanford White's talent. Early photographs show large airy rooms, with the walls covered in either painted stucco, pine, or

(3) The Newport Casino, courtyard. *Sheldon, Artistic Country-Seats*

canvas duck. Furniture was a mixture of heavy Victorian, wicker, and thin-legged English Art furniture.

Passing through the entrance arch to the horseshoe court, the visitor entered a landscape composed of shingles, spindels and balustrades. The contrast of solid and void, of textured surfaces and dark cavities created by the piazzas gave the sense of refuge from the glare of summertime sun. The interwoven balustrades and spindels treated as screens defined a horizontal spatial flow and luminescent boundary. The courtyard came from White's hand; (*Figure 3*) McKim had designed the facade. The whimsical bell-shaped roof on the clock tower, the involved details, are evidence of his eye for ornament. Here, the nervous tension of summer time fun is caught: the smack of a tennis ball, the "ompahpah" of Mullaly's band dressed in scarlet and blue, or the flicker at night of Japanese lanterns in a piazza.

The casino or Music Hall at Short Hills, New Jersey (commissioned in November 1879, and built in 1880) differed from the Newport Casino in size, but not in purpose. (*Figure 4*) Short Hills, New Jersey, was founded in 1877 by Stewart Hartshorne, a wealthy win-

(4) The Short Hills Casino, Short Hills, New Jersey, McKim, Mead & White, architects. *Sheldon, Artistic Country-Seats*

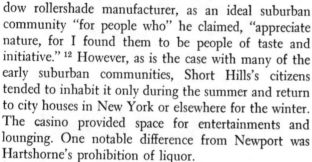

(5) The Narragansett Pier Casino, Narragansett Pier, R. I., McKim, Mead & White, architects. *Sheldon, Artistic Country-Seats*

(6) The Stockbridge Casino, Stockbridge, Mass. McKim, Mead & White, architects. *Picturesque Berkshire*

dow rollershade manufacturer, as an ideal suburban community "for people who" he claimed, "appreciate nature, for I found them to be people of taste and initiative." [12] However, as is the case with many of the early suburban communities, Short Hills's citizens tended to inhabit it only during the summer and return to city houses in New York or elsewhere for the winter. The casino provided space for entertainments and lounging. One notable difference from Newport was Hartshorne's prohibition of liquor.

The style of the Short Hills Casino was described by a critic as an example of the "modern English, with no traces of the Norman and but few of colonial," or in other words, an American adaptation of the Queen Ann.[13] With the shingles, red brick base, and uncanonical usage of classical details, the design of the casino is frequently credited to White but actually it represents the interweaving of his and McKim's sensibilities. The high dominant gable and strong emphatic form reflects McKim's influence, while the more decorative features of the sunflower encrusted pilasters, the shell pediment, the elliptical window, the panels in the gable and the tower represent White's sensibility. The whimsy of the tower especially has the air of White's hand with the round base that supports a gable roof. The critic Montgomery Schuyler described the tower's purpose as "picturesque . . . (but) irrelevant to any other purpose." [14] The interior was essentially one large hall with a stage and dressing rooms at one end and an arcade around the walls. The details of spindels, chamfered edges, green paint with gold trim, led another observer to call the interior "Eastlake."[15]

Indicating a shifting emphasis in McKim, Mead and White's architecture away from the lighter more whimsical features towards greater monumentality and heavi-

ness, is their Narragansett Pier Casino of 1883–1886. (*Figure 5*) Narragansett Pier across the bay from Newport was a rival resort, though as one writer noted: "The habitues of the place are, in general, people of the same social standing as those of Newport, and have in the main less money." [16] Rising only a few feet from the waters edge were high rough-faced ashlar towers that carried the fifty foot arch that spanned the roadway. The origin of the arch lay with the towers of the Loire Valley and European City Gate. Piled on top of the dark void of an open air cafe were highpitched roofs carrying dormers, belfries and lookouts. The roofs were described by a *Harper's Weekly* correspondent as "irregularly rounded and dented to suggest the effect of ravaging winds," and reportedly at the completion of construction McKim had climbed out on the roof and pried up some of the shingles to further the effect of wear.[17] The impact was one of age, of a battered structure that had withstood the forces of nature and man.

The archway, in spite of its appearance, acted as an appendage to the main portion of the casino, a long wooden structure which swept out to the side in grounds that were designed by Frederick Law Olmsted.[18] On several levels were stores, dining rooms and cafes, a billiard room, a theater, and lounge rooms. Informally accessible from a variety of points, piazzas opened off of nearly all levels and created dark ribbons of flowing space that contrasted with the textured shingles and rough stone. Appropriately, the wooden portions of the casino were destroyed by fire and hurricanes fifty years ago, leaving the towers and arch standing alone, ruins of a different lifestyle.

The Stockbridge Casino of 1887 in the Berkshire Hills of Western Massachusetts, while far smaller than the Narragansett Pier Casino, continues the shifting emphasis towards a greater historical presence and more of an elite image. (*Figure 6*) McKim, Mead & White were well known in the Berkshires, having designed a number of summer homes, and in Stockbridge, specifically, St. Paul's Church, a donation of Prescott Hall Butler who served on the board of directors of the casino, and a house for Joseph H. Choate, who also belonged to the casino's board. A sense of envy perhaps, can be felt in the words of the author of *Picturesque Berkshire:*

The church was designed by Mr. McKim—so was the Casino. The Casino is an awful innovation—a new departure of the most pronounced type. These are sadly degenerate days. Our forebears found amusement for themselves. Their descendants, forsooth, must have their amusements provided for them. The elect few dance in the Casino every Saturday night.[19]

With the Stockbridge commission, McKim, who was the designer, turned to the precedent of early American architecture and created an image reminescent of a Georgian town hall. Rectangular in shape with a projecting arcaded loggia, the detailing and paint (yellow with white trim) was avowedly eighteenth century in inspiration. The interior contained a lounge for women, a billiard room, a reading room, a conversation room, a kitchen and a two story hall for music and entertainments.

The Colonial Revival image presented in the Stockbridge Casino is directly analogous to the direction McKim, Mead & White were taking in their domestic house designs such as the Taylor or Edgar houses in Newport, or in public buildings, the more formal neo-Renaissance image of the Boston Public Library. Significantly, McKim designed the Stockbridge Casino simultaneously with the Boston Library.[20]

Casino designs by McKim, Mead & White for a few years after Stockbridge Casino are not so significant. In Babylon, a summer spot on the south side of Long Island, they created in 1888 a small shingle covered dance casino, which disappeared years ago. Back in Narragansett Pier, the firm did several proposals for Louis Sherry, the New York restauranteur who had purchased the Narragansett Pier Casino. A casino incorporating a bathing pavilion was erected for Sherry after the turn-of-the-century but it has long disappeared.[21]

Finally, there is one casino design by McKim, Mead and White that indicates the complete evolution of the American resort casino, both socially and architecturally. In 1902 McKim, Mead & White (with Stanford White as the chief designer) were commissioned by John Jacob Astor IV to design a casino for his summer place, Ferncliff on the Hudson at Rhinebeck. White had previously made some additions to the house at Rhinebeck as well as other work for the Astor family in New York and Newport. The casino was essentially a gift by John Jacob Astor, IV, a tall, somewhat bumbling and dreamy person, to his wife, Ava Willing, well known for her beauty, ego and passion for bridge and tennis.[22] White's design, built in 1902–1905, was for a private sports and entertainment casino. Lounges were provided for bridge and parties; there were dressing rooms, guest rooms for bachelor guests, an indoor swimming pool, and a large enclosed tennis court. (*Figure 7*) The tennis court with Guastavino vaulting and a skylight was Roman in scale.

(7)   The Astor Casino, Rhinebeck, New York, McKim, Mead & White, architects. *A Monograph of the Works of McKim, Mead & White*

Sited on top of a hill and first viewed at a distance from the drive, the Astor Casino gives the initial impression of temple form. Upon approach, though, the temple form splits into two functional parts: the tennis court and the lounges and dressing rooms. Stylistically, Stanford White adopted for the facade a French Renaissance idiom of a recessed loggia and delicate Ionic columns and pilasters that recalled the Grand Trianon at Versailles. Moving to the rear, from which a spectacular view of the Hudson River could be gained, the building emerges far out of the ground with an imperialistic disdain. A pompous historical image was created, an irony that was not lost at the time. A critic writing for the *Architectural Record* noted the appropriateness of using styles from the time of Marie Antoinette to house games of millionaires in the twentieth century, though he felt Ava Astor's games were perhaps "more wholesome." [23] Unfortunately for John and Ava Astor, their later life was not so happy; they were divorced in 1910, and he died in the Titanic disaster of 1912.

McKim, Mead & White were not the only casino architects in America. Peabody & Stearns, the Boston firm, produced the low lying Elberon (New Jersey) Casino that disappeared years ago.[24] There were casinos or analogous structures at most of the resorts: Cape May, Seabright, Tuxedo Park and Lake Minnetonka, for example. But in most cases, the architects are little known or forgotten and the buildings either altered or destroyed. Certainly none of them appear to challenge McKim, Mead & White's pre-eminence as the leading designers of casinos. At the time it was so recognized. In 1886 George William Sheldon in *Artistic Country Seats*, reviewed a number of the casinos and claimed:

As a source of aesthetic pleasure, the country clubhouse in the United States is scarcely more than eight years old. Its beginning may be traced to the Newport Casino—designed by Messrs. McKim, Mead and White.[25]

A comment should be made on the fate of the resort casino. Of those reviewed herein, all are either gone or heavily altered and changed in purpose. Only the Newport Casino remains in somewhat its original form, but it is now a private tennis club and museum. There is no longer dancing or strolling on the piazza. It is a dinosaur, a relic of leisurely summers. The resort casino did produce an offspring. As people continued to desert the city, seeking the good life and a year round vacation in the suburbs, the casino in the guise of the country club followed along. As the summer resort cottage is the ancestor of the suburban home, the casino is the forebear of the country club. But that is another story.

The paradigm of the change from the semi-public Newport Short Hills and Narragansett Casinos to the private Stockbridge Casino and ultimately personal Astor Casino indicates the increasing privatism and social stratification of the turn-of-the-century period. The difference in images indicates this shift, from the informal easy flow of the Newport Casino through the growing heaviness and pretentiousness of the Narragansett and Stockbridge casinos to the final solution at Rhinebeck where a pompous formality becomes the image. The forms appear to fit the lifestyles contained therein.

NOTES

[1] *The Oxford English Dictionary* (New York, 1971), p. 348.

[2] The Canfield Casino at Saratoga Springs was the one significant American gambling casino. However, the building was originally erected as a private house, and consequently is not included in this survey.

[3] Published in *The New York Sketch Book of Architecture*, III (November 1876), p. 43.

[4] For background information, see: Richard Guy Wilson, "The Early Work of Charles F. McKim," *Winterthur Portfolio*, Vol. 14, No. 3 (Fall 1979); Richard Guy Wilson, "Charles F. McKim and the Rise of the Renaissance in America," (Ph.D. dissertation, University of Michigan, 1972); Charles Moore, *The Life and Times of Charles Follen McKim* (Boston and New York, 1929); and Charles Baldwin, *Stanford White* (New York, 1931).

[5] New York Times (8 February 1878).

[6] *Dictionary of American Biography*, Vol. 1, pp. 199–202. Maud Howe Elliott, *This was my Newport* (Cambridge, 1944), pp.

153–54. An interesting portrait of Bennett is given in Gore Vidal, *1876* (New York, 1976).

[7] Newport Mercury (30 August 1879). See also, Richard O'Connor, *The Golden Summers, An Antic History of Newport* (New York, 1974), pp. 103–105.

[8] Newport Mercury (25 October 1879, 7 November 1879, 6 December 1879, and 10 January 1880).

[9] Originally, the Newport Casino had bachelors apartments but they were removed in a remodelling of 1881 by McKim, Mead & White, and converted into a billiard room.

[10] Richmond Barrett, *Good Old Summer Days* (New York, 1952).

[11] The Queen Anne background is covered in Vincent Scully, Jr., *The Shingle Style* (New Haven, 1955). Shaw's Tabard Inn and Stores at Bedford Park, outside London, have the closest resemblance to the Newport Casino. They were published in *The Builder*, 38 (2 January 1880), p. 10.

[12] Quoted in The New York Times (13 January 1937), p. 18. See also, "An American Park," *The American Architect and Building News*, 16 (12 July 1884), pp. 15–16.

[13] George William Sheldon, *Artistic Country-Seats* (New York, 1886), p. 116.

[14] Montgomery Schuyler, "Some Suburbs of New York, I: New Jersey," *Lippincott's Magazine*, 8 (July 1884), p. 23.

[15] "Suburban Homes—Short Hills," *Frank Leslie's Illustrated Newspaper* (13 November 1880), p. 80. After years of disuse, the casino became the Short Hills Racquet Club and survived until the spring of 1978 when it was destroyed by fire.

[16] "Narragansett and its Casino," *Harper's Weekly*, 31 (27 August 1887), p. 611.

[17] Ibid. and C. H. Reilly, *McKim, Mead & White* (London, 1924), p. 20.

[18] Letter, W. R. Mead to F. L. Olmsted, 20 March 1884, Library of Congress, Manuscript Room, Olmsted Collection. Frederick Law Olmsted, Jr. and Theodora Kimball, eds., *Frederick Law Olmsted, Landscape Architect, 1822–1903* (New York, 1922), vol. 1, p. 27.

[19] *Picturesque Berkshire, Part II, South* (Northampton, Mass., 1893), p. 34. Information on the Board of Directors is found in *Berkshire Courier* (11 May 1887).

[20] Drawings for the Stockbridge Casino are in The New York Historical Society, Map & Print Room, McKim, Mead & White Collection. They are dated April and May 1887, and one is signed, "McKim, Mead & White—Boston Office, 53 Beacon Street." This is the office McKim set up for the Boston Public Library project.

[21] Letter, McKim, Mead & White, Bert Fenner to John H. Hanan, 16 September 1916, The New York Historical Society notes the different work the firm did for Sherry. Additionally at least one set of plans survives at The New York Historical Society.

[22] Harvey O'Connor, *The Astors* (New York, 1941), pp. 251–53, Lucy Kavaler, *The Astors, A Family Chronicle* (London, 1966), pp. 141–43.

[23] "Court and Pool at Ferncliff," *The Architectural Record*, 18 (July 1905), p. 26. The writer was probably Herbert Croly. The Astor Casino in the 1950s became the home of the Carmelite Sisters for their Ferncliff Nursing Home. In recent years, it has been threatened with destruction.

[24] Sheldon, *Artistic Country-Seats*, II, pp. 101–104.

[25] Ibid., p. 101.

RUSTIC CONNOTATIONS:
FURNISHING NATIONAL PARK HOSTELRIES

Rodd L. Wheaton

RUSTIC CONNOTATIONS:
FURNISHING NATIONAL PARK HOSTELRIES

Rodd L. Wheaton

VISITING A NATIONAL PARK was, and still is, an experience. Since its establishment in 1872 as America's first national park, Yellowstone has long ranked as the ultimate park experience, a chance to tour the "stinking waters." From the beginning overnight accommodations were an integral part of the experience.

Conrad Kohrs wrote in his *Autobiography* that, in 1883, he drove his family through Yellowstone in the ranch daughtery wagon accompanied by a four-horse provision wagon. Kohrs continued by noting: "We were well equipped with tents, beddings, and provisions and camped from the time we started until we reached home." [1]

However, the Kohrs family were "Sagebrushers," not to be confused with real "tourists" classified appropriately as dudes, dudenes, and dudettes.

Tourists arrived in Yellowstone principally as guests of the Northern Pacific Railroad for a five-day side trip. Met at the spur line terminus, talleyho stagecoaches transported the tourists through the Roosevelt Arch to the first stop: the National Hotel at Mammoth Hot Springs. Begun in 1883, the same year as Kohrs' visit, the hotel was designed by L. F. Buffington of St. Paul, Minnesota, for the Yellowstone Park Improvement Company. The 151-room frame structure, a shingled Queen Anne-Tudor pile, was incongruous on the landscape. With its large lobby, its dining room complete with two French chefs and a German baker, and its bar and a barber shop, all lit with electric arc lights, the hotel clearly was aping eastern spa architecture associated with "taking the waters."

National Hotel, which suffered through numerous financial difficulties and was finally demolished in 1935, was furnished in 1883 at a cost of $60,000.[2] Remnants of Colonial Revival golden oak furnishings, such as the lobby clock and writing desks and chairs, remain to sug-

gest the decoration—a far cry from the rustic style as purported by A. J. Davis, or William C. Wicks in his *Log Cabins and How to Build and Furnish Them*, published in 1889, and at such Adirondack camps as William Durrant's Camp Pineknot at Raquette Lake, New York. All remain a testament to the fascination with mock-primitive. At Yellowstone, beyond the confines of Mammoth Hot Springs, however, real primitive was the rule. Frame and tent structures offered meager accommodations. Of the appropriately named Shack Hotel, not dissimilar from the first Canyon Hotel, one disgruntled tourist wrote "the rooms are canvas, formed with a flap for a door. A deal bed, small table, and a wash bowl with a four by six looking glass furnish the accommodations." [3] Another visitor noted that pine stumps stuck "conveniently out of the ground" to provide seating.[4]

More substantial barracks-like structures were soon constructed at each major overnight stop. This included the second hotel at Canyon, a three-story frame building with little distinction beyond a minimal porte-cochere at the entrance centered on the symmetrical facade.[4] Accommodating, but hardly inviting.

By 1903, a year which boasted 13,165 visitors,[5] it was apparent that there was a need to be more inviting, particularly at Old Faithful Geyser, the most popular park attraction. Old Faithful Inn, built during the winter of 1903–1904 was designed by Robert C. Reamer for the Yellowstone Park Company, a Northern Pacific subsidiary, is basically symmetrical in plan with a 93-foot-high lobby flanked by east and west wings. All is painfully contorted to look asymmetrical with assorted dormers and gables and crazy-quilt window sash. Logs, stone, cedar shingles, and knarled and burreled railings, braces and brackets were used freely to convey a sense of the forest primeval—wilderness—Yellowstone National Park.

Based on Adirondack precedents it could be assumed that such a rustic monument should be furnished with equally rustic furniture. Not true. Instead, company President Harry W. Child, opted for the purchase of Arts and Crafts or Mission Style oak furnishings, along with additional equipment, at a total cost of over $28,000, from an unnamed manufacturer in New York state. At the same time Child itemized purchases of "Old Hickory Chairs and Valise Benches," "Black Rockers," wash stands, and scarves for the company's other hotels.[6]

Though not necessarily rustic (Figure 1) the use of Arts and Crafts-Mission Style furniture at Old Faithful Inn, supposedly one of the world's largest log buildings, would have had the approval of Gustav Stickley. Stickley wrote in 1911 in reference to furnishing log houses that "craftsman" furniture was in "harmony with nature and its unity of the best civilization with the best in cruder forms of life." [7]

Typically the lobby space, the product of railroad trestle builders, was furnished with arm chairs, wing back chairs, rockers, settles, and side chairs of several design variations arranged in groups and around the massive fireplace chimney obelisk, itself a repository for a handforged copper and iron clock.

The floor was laid with large Indian style rugs which again appear to anticipate Stickley who later wrote "that Indian products are becoming more or less fashionable." Stickley noted that:

It is the quality of sincerity that gives the Indian blanket its peculiar value when used as a rug, portier or couch cover in a Craftsman room, or in any one of the rooms so characteristic of the West. No form of drapery harmonizes quite so well with plain, sturdy forms in woodwork and furniture and with the mellow tones of the natural wood, as do these Indian blankets, for the reason that they are simply another expression of the same idea.[8]

Within the guest rooms of Old Faithful Inn (Figure 2) the decoration was influenced, if not dominated by, the log slab wall and ceiling treatment. One Mrs. E. H. Johnson, a hotel guest in 1905, wrote:

And then we came to the Inn, the most unique and perfect place; it is the craftsman's dream realized. My room alone is a paradise of restfullness though in a rough and rustic fashion. The barred windows which open as a lattice and the figured curtains; the furniture is green stained; the red slat-seats and backs to the chairs and the bed a four poster iron with white valance; the walls, rough pine boards, and even the lights carry out the design.[9]

Much of the described furniture remains at the Inn, though the "upgrading" of rooms has taken a toll and produced curiosities. A copper topped washstand, stained green, is now a lobby console table. A drop fronted bureau is relegated to an entrance vestibule. A slat seat chair is upholstered in vinyl.

Stepping into the dining room in 1905, Mrs. Johnson again observed, "At luncheon we had another treat. The dining room has its own charm with its red palm bean figured draperies, blue dishes and brass and copper accessories."[10] (Blue Willow ware was long a favorite for place settings, though railroad insignia china was used in the early days.) At lunch one thing Mrs. Johnson did miss was the chamber orchestra normally stationed in musicians gallery during the evening meal.

By the late teens, the Old Faithful Inn dining room had been rearranged with individual tables, but the rustic hickory side chairs with woven hickory splint seating and backing were retained. In 1904 these chairs were an early use in a western hotel of what was essentially considered porch furniture, too crude for interior use where more fashionable Mission furniture, combined with Indian rugs, suggested the rustic. More typically fanciful hickory and willow were used on the Inn's terraces in the more traditional manner. (Figure 3)

Simultaneously, with the completion of the Old Faithful Inn, the barracks-like 1889 Lake Hotel was remodeled, possibly also under the direction of Robert Reamer.[11] If Reamer was the architect, he certainly proved himself to be a proper eclectic master with the addition of Colonial Revival Ionic porticoes. The resultant building was totally unrelated to Yellowstone National Park in form or materials, all painted yellow and trimmed white.

The interior architectural distinction is the glazed tile fireplace of the registration lobby. In the dining room, rattan chairs along with "fish-bowl" on Ionic column light fixtures provided some visual interest in an otherwise bland public space. (Figure 4) Similarly, rattan and wicker were used in the lounge relating to the solarium aspect of the space. Angular in form, possibly originally complementing mission oak, the wicker is all far removed from the rustic connotations just created a few miles away at Old Faithful. Saratoga prevailed; the West be damned.

In 1910 Reamer was back at work for the Yellowstone Park Company designing and supervising the construction of Canyon Hotel. Though the rustic style epitomized by Old Faithful Inn was again ignored, Reamer created a structure that was, at least, responsive to its site overlooking the Grand Canyon of the Yellow-

(1)   The Lobby, Old Faithful Inn, Yellowstone National Park, 1905.   Detroit Publishing Co. photo, Colorado Historical Society

(2)   Guest Room 46, Old Faithful Inn, Yellowstone National Park, circa 1915.   Haynes Foundation Collection, Montana Historical Society

(5)   The Lounge, Canyon Hotel (demolished),
Yellowstone National Park, circa 1915. *Haynes
Foundation Collection, Montana Historical Society*

stone River. This was the same site that proved un-
stable in 1964 necessitating the hotel's demolition. In
any event, it is obvious that Reamer was by 1910 well
aware of the developments of the Prairie School of
Architecture. The low profile, horizontal building,
which encompasses much Chicago influence, encloses
several large public spaces including the 84′ x 175′ lounge.
Notably the lounge light fixtures were Wrightian in
concept contrasting with the gigantic scissor truss roof
system. However, the furnishings, as seen in a circa
1920 view, (*Figure 5*) are more typical of the period
—wicker and upholstered easy chairs—undoubtedly installed to enhance the design of the Lounge, "the salient
feature of the new Canyon Hotel." Here, it was intended that the guests "were to see and be seen, to
witness the proud pagentry of the promenade, to study
character and apparel and to gossip and to listen to
music." [12]

In the lobby light oak furnishings, described as the
"Flanders Style" with turned supports, were used to
line the walls and buttress the columns in deference to
the standard hotel lobby decor. Minimal rustic consid-

(3)   "Cosy Corner on West Veranda, Old Faithful Inn,
Yellowstone National Park," circa 1905. *Detroit
Publishing Co. photo, Colorado Historical Society*

(4)   The Dining Room, Lake Hotel, Yellowstone
National Park, circa 1920. *Haynes Foundation
Collection, Montana Historical Society*

erations probably resulted in the purchase of the line
from "Limbert's Arts Crafts Furniture" of Grand Rap-
ids. Limbert also produced the dining room chairs
(*Figure 6*) which remarkably reflect a commercial pro-
duction of Frank Lloyd Wright's early designs. For the
moment the taste of the hotel concessioner anticipated
the visitor, and was modified by the mid-1930s with the
installation of birch veneered moderne furniture bear-
ing labels from the Algoma Plywood and Veneer Co.,
Algoma, Wisconsin. Included were club sofas, now re-
upholstered and forgotten at Lake Hotel, pedestal tables,
and writing desk and chairs.

(6)   The Dining Room, Canyon Hotel (demolished),
       Yellowstone National Park, circa 1915.   *Haynes
       Foundation Collection, Montana Historical Society*

In other western areas concessioners were developing the parks at a similar pace with the intent of parting
the tourist from his dollar with minimal discomfort.
On the south rim of Grand Canyon the Atchison
Topeka & Santa Fe Railroad, in concert with the Fred
Harvey Company, built in 1905–1906 the El Tovar Hotel. Designed by Charles Whittlesley of Topeka, the
building was described by the promotional literature as
"Swiss Chalet and Norway Villa" in style.[13] Such
flaunted eclecticism included a 15th century style dining room with Indian murals; "art rooms" containing
Thomas Moran paintings, and Indian rugs, baskets and
pottery; and a log lined lobby. The hotel's proximity to
the southwest Indian tribes contributed much to the
inclusion of Indian objects as accessories in a cake icing
decor in an attempt to pass off a "Rube Goldberg-
esque" building as rustic.

(7)   The Lobby, Many Glacier Hotel, Glacier National
       Park, circa 1920.   *Photo reproduced from a
       clipping in a 1923 scrap book*

(8) The Lobby, Paradise Inn, Mount Ranier National
Park, circa 1925. *National Park Service*

Near the Canadian border the Great Northern Railway was instrumental in the development of Glacier National Park, established in 1910. Outside the east entrance to the park the railroad constructed Glacier Park Hotel in 1913. The following year, within the park, Many Glacier Hotel was under construction to the design of Thomas McMahan of St. Paul, Minnesota, and J. J. Hill, President of the Great Northern. Hill believed that the northern rockies were the Alps of America and naturally opted for Swiss architecture; hence, the construction of a giant Swiss Chalet, dubbed "Big Trees Lodge" by the neighboring Blackfoot Indians. The hotel, with its massive naos space central lobby, *(Figure 7)* similar to Glacier Park Hotel, was described in 1923 as "an immense timbered structure in perfect harmony with its mountainous background." [14]

Since the hotel has been swept clean of original furniture, it is difficult to ascertain the problem of furnishing a large Swiss chalet. The solution, in part, at Many Glacier was to include details for tables, bedsteads, and cabinetry within the 142 sheets of construction drawings. These pieces were to be built on site, and augmented with Mission style seating furniture such as seen in an early view of the Glacier Park Hotel lobby. Stickley and others had long advocated the do-it-yourself aspects of craftsman furniture. For Many Glacier Hotel it was easy to build and it was in style in 1915. But, in reality, craftsman furniture had little to do with bell boys in lederhousen, and the addition of Colonial Windsor and bamboo splint chairs. The furniture, but hardly the building design, did, though, relate to the 180' canvas mural painted by Medicine Owl depicting Blackfoot tribal history, the lobby's copper hooded firepit, Indian motif rugs, and, to a lesser extent, considering the period's interest in particularly Japanese prints, Japanese lantern light fixtures and a Japanese couple in native dress serving afternoon tea on the hotel's verandah. Completing the lobby decor, the balconies provided a suitable display for, litteraly, the trappings of the West—the ultimate statement of the rustic, the conquering and subjugation of nature with or without Teddy Roosevelt's approval.

Porch furniture, like that of the smaller more intimate Lake McDonald Lodge built in 1914, was rustic pine and hickory rockers and armchairs typically with woven hickory splint seating and backing.

In addition to the Prince of Wales Hotel at Waterton Lakes National Park in Canada, Glacier National Park provided yet another visitor experience: back country lodging such as at the Granite Park Chalet designed by Samuel L. Bartlett and built in 1914. Examination of the Great Northern archives dealing with the Belton Chalet suggests typical room furnishings of the hotels where all that remains are rustic rope fire escapes. Included were brass beds, such as bedsteads at Sperry Chalet; oak rockers with canned seats; and oak dressers. Rustic rockers and arm chairs were also listed and probably were intended for porch furniture.[15]

The relegation of rustic furniture to the porch was reconsidered with the furnishings of Mount Ranier National Park's Paradise Inn, designed by Heath and Gove of Tacoma, Washington, and built 1916–17.[16] The massive log frame building is distinctly rustic in design as compared to its "Swiss-esque" predecessor at Many Glacier. Because of this break from historicism, the architects apparently felt that Paradise Inn merited furniture to complement the interior. The scale of commercially available hickory was inappropriate, necessitating designing log furniture for the public spaces. (Figure 8) Included were log tables, a grandfather clock, a piano, and chairs. The pointed log ends lend a Gothic air, though back crest rails suggest Northern European folk design. More traditional seating was used conventionally in the dining room. Typically, Navajo rugs were draped from balconies and, in a novel application, wrapped around columns. Like the Glacier hotels, Japanese lanterns seemed to be a natural adjunct to log columns.

In the 1920s the automobile began to change the course of the hotel building in the national parks. As elsewhere, the public sought accommodations in motor courts. The luxury was to drive to one's private wilderness cabin after having registered in the main lodge which usually contained the dining room and the proverbial gift shop. Such was the guest experience at Bryce Canyon Lodge built in 1925 and 1927 and designed by Los Angeles Architect Gilbert Stanley Underwood for the Utah Parks Company, a subsidiary of the Union Pacific Railroad.

As originally conceived the design of the lodge was far removed from historicism and attempted to provide a rustic environment emphasized by undulating shingles, stone masonry, wrought iron fittings, and (Figure 9) the interior installation of woven Indian-motif draperies, hickory furniture from the Old Hickory Company, Martinsville, Indiana, and log light fixtures. Indian rugs covered the floors and paved the way to the gift shop where guests could purchase the proof of their visit.

At Bryce Canyon Lodge the original guest cabins were rather simply furnished with plain bedsteads and director's chairs.[17] These cabins, in 1928, were augmented with deluxe cabins furnished with fake wicker furniture from Kaltex Furniture, Jackson, Michigan, patented in 1916, and woven draperies suggestive of southwest heritage.

In 1926, Underwood designed a lodge for the Utah Parks Company at Zion National Park in a similar style to Bryce Canyon Lodge and similarly furnished. Underwood's design for the Zion Lodge set the tone for his Ahwahnee Hotel built in 1927 for the Yosemite Park and Curry Company at Yosemite National Park and the Grand Canyon Hotel built on the North Rim in 1928. The latter, was rebuilt after a fire in 1935. The Ahwahnee, however, remains as a testimony to the premanence of concrete logs and stone buttressing.[18] The interiors remain the best example of the fruition of the use of American Indian motifs. (Figure 10)

(9) **The Lobby, Bryce Canyon Lodge, Bryce Canyon National Park, circa 1930.** *Union Pacific Historical Papers, Nebraska State Historical Society*

(10) **The Lobby, Ahwahnee Hotel, Yosemite National Park, circa 1945.** *National Park Service*

Basically, the designs are integrated into the decor. Indian objects were no longer just draped or laid down, they were stenciled on columns and walls and incorporated into stained glass. Inspiration was taken from all the Indian arts with primary emphasis being of California Pima and Pomo basketry. Complementing the Indian decor are Spanish Colonial seating furniture as a tribute to pioneer Californians, a heretofore unexplored aspect of rustic connotations. Certainly rustic hotel construction and furnishing in the national parks reached its zenith with the completion of the Ahwahnee.

In retrospect, though Old Faithful Inn remains as a premiere monument to rustic architecture in America, its furnishings were merely the best of the period with little direct relationship to the architecture beyond accepted aesthetics of the day. Canyon Hotel certainly was innovative, but the building, while relating to its site, is far from the traditional concept of rustic. Wicker and rattan furnishings, while significant, were modified by the installation of the modern pieces.

Glacier Park hotels relied on the shock appeal to convey wilderness. Taxidermy and a myriad Japanese lanterns crowd the lobbies which are essentially monumental classical architectural spaces that in turn rendered furnishings insignificant.

It took Paradise Inn to begin to define rustic. The scale of the individual pieces of furniture, while relating to spaces to be filled, have, however, a strange full-scale dollhouse quality.

However, by the late 1920s rustic furnishings for rustic appeal came into its own. Rustic hickory, willow and pine furniture moved indoors. A more sophisticated traveling public expected their accommodations to be rustic in line with the "Smoky-the-Bear" image created by the Park Service on the foundation of the park concessioners who long were peddling Indian artifacts as genuine rustic souveniers. It took the construction of the Ahwahnee Hotel to fully realize that objects, beyond beign merely accessories, could be design inspiration and define rustic connotations for furnishing National Park hostelries.

NOTES

[1] Conrad K. Warren (ed.). *Conrad Kohrs: An Autobiography* (Deer Lodge, MT: C. K. Warren, 1977), p. 77.

[2] Aubrey L. Haines. *The Yellowstone Story*, Vol 2 (Yellowstone National Park: Yellowstone Library and Museum Association, 1977), p. 272.

[3] Susan C. Scofield and Jeremy C. Schmidt. *The Inn at Old Faithful* ... (Bozeman, MT: Crowsnest Associates, 1979), pp. 5–6.

[4] Haines, Vol. 1, p. 276.

[5] Scofield, p. 4.

[6] Minnesota Historical Society, St. Paul, MN. Division of Archives and Manuscripts, Northern Pacific Railroad Records, President's Subject file No. 210A, folder 10, "Yellowstone Park Association, Amounts Expended in Improvements and Betterments, Season 1904."

[7] Gustav Stickley. *The Best of Craftsman Homes* (Santa Barbara: Peregrine Smith, Inc., 1979), p. 89.

[8] Barry Sanders (ed.). *The Craftsman, An Anthology* (Santa Barbara: Peregrine Smith, Inc., 1978), p. 227.

[9] Scofield, p. 23.

[10] *Ibid.*

[11] William Bemet was cited in 1900 as having designed additions for Lake Hotel according to the research of Berle Clemensen, Historian, National Park Service, Denver Service Center.

[12] J. H. Raftery. *A Miracle in Hotel Building, The Dramatic Story of the Building of the New Canyon Hotel in Yellowstone Park*, Yellowstone National Park: Yellowstone Park Co., n.d., p. 9.

[13] William C. Tweed, Laura E. Soulliere, and Henry G. Law. *National Park Service, Rustic Architecture: 1916–1942* (San Francisco: National Park Service, Western Regional Office, Division of Cultural Resource Management, 1977), p. 8.

[14] Glacier National Park clipping, Miss Adrienne Bush Vacation Scrapbook, 1923, on loan from Colorado Railroad Museum to National Park Service, Rocky Mountain Region.

[15] Minnesota Historical Society. Glacier Park Co., Box 1991, Belton Chalets.

[16] David E. Snow. *Mount Ranier Paradise Inn, Historic Structure Report* (Denver, CO: National Park Service, Denver Service Center, 1977), p. 6.

[17] Union Pacific System. *Zion, Grand Canyon, Bryce Canyon National Parks, the Cedar Breaks, Kaibab National Forest* (Omaha, NE: Union Pacific System, 1931), p. 41.

[18] Tweed, et. al., p. 44.